To Jean.

Wishing you a very happy
Birthday

Love Ruth

THE
MOST SUCCESSFUL
NATION

IN THE HISTORY OF THE WORLD

John Hawkins

authorHOUSE®

AuthorHouse™ UK Ltd.
500 Avebury Boulevard
Central Milton Keynes, MK9 2BE
www.authorhouse.co.uk
Phone: 08001974150

First published by AuthorHouse 12/17/2009

ISBN: 978-1-4490-5682-7 (sc)

Front cover:
The Secret of England's Greatness
*(Queen Victoria presenting a Bible
in the Audience Chamber at Windsor)
by Thomas Jones Barker c 1863*
© National Portrait Gallery, London.

Bible references from the New International Version of the Bible.

This book is printed on acid-free paper.

Contents

To

NICOLA
OLIVER
SAM

Preface

Why write a book with the title "The Most Successful Nation in the History of the World"? There is something unseemly in puffing up one nation over and above all others – some might say possibly dangerous. But I believe it is overdue and the reason is the rise of the cult of multiculturalism and its parent postmodernism. Multiculturalism is a recent ideology – the word does not even appear in the Chambers Twentieth Century Dictionary my parents gave me in 1961. It is a very slippery concept and it seems each culture has its own definition.

Multiculturalism might best be described as a collection of diverse cultures and identities, distinct yet equal in value but with an overarching common thread of historical national identity, accepted and respected by everyone and which holds society together.

This definition might hold if all contributing cultures accepted the idea of the overarching common culture. Unfortunately multiculturalism nurtures within itself the seeds of its own destruction. It needs only one of the distinct entities to reject the overarching culture for social collapse to become a possibility.

Also, some bodies claim that the eradication of inequalities, particularly race discrimination, must be a tackled as a priority. This invariably means that a minority group has a grievance against a native white population. Supporters of multiculturalism will then regard the native culture as deficient and it becomes no longer the overarching common thread to be admired and nurtured, but a threat to be broken and discarded.

This has been the pattern in recent decades; historical national values being distorted and disdained with the negative being emphasised. It is my desire to try and redress the balance.

Postmodernism saturated with atheistic secular humanism and[1] closely related to multiculturalism, in the western world dominates the cultural and intellectual high ground of our age. It is a phenomenon which encompasses political and social philosophy. Its denial of objectivity results in unleashing of ideologies which by definition operate outside of any moral constraint and in its social manifestation tends to nurture victimhood, grievance and envy.

Many people are beginning to agree with Ivan Massow who said, "I'm about ready for some form and substance" on resigning from the chairmanship of the Institute of Contemporary Art, after describing conceptual art as

---

[1] Since objectivity is an illusion, science according to the ideological argument, subverts oppressed groups,   females, ethnics, third-world peoples (Melford Spiro 1996).

"self indulgent craft less tat"[2]. Maybe the intellectual climate is changing!

John Hawkins, Totnes

December 2009

[2]   The Times Saturday 9th February 2002

Introduction

Where there is no vision the people perish.

Proverbs chapter 29 verse 18 Authorised Version of the Bible

Where there is no revelation, the people cast off restraint.

Proverbs chapter 29 verse 18 New International Version

In the opening years of the twenty first century there is a sense that many nations in the western world have lost their way. It seems that the principles of liberty and pursuit of happiness are too difficult for ordinary folk to struggle after and are best abdicated to the state to be managed by those who can be paid a comfortable wage to carry out the directions of those who know what is best for us.

By some, this drift is seen as the evolution of a society which is moving ever onward and upward to a better state. Any criticism suggesting standards are not as good as they should be is answered by the implied statement "We've never had it so good".

There is a brittleness in the intellectual fabric which can only be kept from rupture by ever more state control of ever more social and personal functions whereby the restrictive almost dead hand of the state stifles individual initiative at an ever increasing cost.

The purpose of this book is to look at history to see that things have been managed differently in the past, to learn and maybe shake off our delusion and inertia.

This malaise, and I think it is a sickness, is mainly because we live in a two dimensional world. We have physical and intellectual dimensions but no spiritual depth. Granted we recognise the intangibles of art and give them a spiritual label, but the possibility that spiritual powers exist beyond and outside human control is disdained. This is denial in a most unhealthy form leaving a vacuum which is filled with all sorts of exotic religions, but most of all filled with the arrogant idolatry of worship of the human intellect.

From the later half of the twentieth century to the first decades of the twenty first it has not been intellectually respectable to bring a belief in God into the public arena. God was confined to precise slots such as 'Songs of Praise' or the 'Thought for the day' on the BBC and maybe a state funeral or a royal celebration. Secular humanism has been promoted unchallenged by the intellectual establishment to the extent that even many professional clergy in the established denominations themselves are diffident about proclaiming their belief in the Christian God. Too many thinkers have been intimidated by the secularist humanistic community who honour their godless agenda before truth.

This book is essentially a collection of free standing essays by a Christian looking at the world from a Christian viewpoint; written by someone who believes that God made human kind in His own image and loves His creation so much that He Himself is willing to face up to human depravity and to pay the immense price necessary to enable us to relate to a God of order, fulfillment, liberty, kindness, justice and love.

This book is a statement of the superlative. It is about the *most* successful nation in history, not *one* of the most successful. It will therefore provoke dissension, maybe passionate dissension, and inevitably the accusation that the selected nation has many failures and weaknesses. But it is my objective to show that this nation stood head and shoulders above any other and to show why.

This book is also a statement of the comparative. No nation, just as no individual, is without fault so compared with the highest standards of behaviour and righteousness even the most successful is a failure. All nations are flawed just as all persons have 'sinned and fallen short of the glory of God'.

It is my aim, even though I am praising one nation above all others, that there should be no place for pride, arrogance, self satisfaction or any sense of moral superiority. I guess the most important characteristic should be humility with some touch of humour.

So an underlining thread throughout this book is the spiritual theme. A peoples relationship to God effects every facet of their lives and this is true for nations as much as for individuals. It is true for believers. It is also true for unbelievers.

Chapter 1

WHICH IS IT?

What definition does one use to determine the most successful nation? There are so many standards that could be used; which has produced the best artists or musicians; which is the kindest or most generous; which is the richest or most powerful? The choice made here is which nation has benefited humanity the most. Which nation has brought prosperity, peace, liberty? Which has given the world the principle that machine energy was better than muscle? Which has exercised raw power in the world in the most benign way? Which has faced up to tyranny and immensely strong dictators for little more than principle?

Using the above, on the basis of which nation has brought most benefits to humanity, there is only one possibility and that is Britain.

It is considered a mystery why such a small island offshore from the mainland of Europe should have such an immense influence in the world – much smaller than either Japan[3] or Madagascar. Even with an unappealing unreliable climate with bleak winters and wet summers people have flocked to this island from all over the world. During the first millennium AD invading peoples from northern Europe pushed the earlier Celtic settlers to the fringes of the island replacing them by Romans, Angles, Saxons, Vikings, Danes, Picts, Scots etc. From earliest times there has been an impressive racial mix. The second millennium has seen a more benign movement of people into the country; French, Dutch, Jewish and latterly Africans, West Indians, Asians etc. coming often to better themselves but sometimes to seek safety from persecution in their homelands.

How could this mishmash of peoples isolated on a small island become such a potent force, mainly for good, in the world? The answer is in what they believed.

It was the Christian faith of significant numbers of people in all walks of life that made Britain the most successful nation in the history of the world.

What you believe is important. Dominating the early twenty first century are the materialists of various shapes – Marxists, humanist secularists etc – whose reluctant patron saint is Charles Darwin. Their belief is in the survival of the fittest. And although they don't actually

---

[3] Nations:

Name	area 1000s sq mile	pop millions
GB	92	60
Japan	152	127
Madagascar	224	19
Taiwan	12	23
Papua NG	175	6

say so, their creed is based on greed, because as for them this life is all there is it is therefore acceptable for them to acquire all they can and only when they are comfortable are they willing to let a few crumbs fall from their table.[4] We see the fruits of this all around us in shabby manipulative government and the worship of money making.

Our society has few absolutes. For example it is commonly understood that there is no absolute truth. What you believe to be true is fine; I probably don't agree with you so my truth is different, but in the interest of tolerance we don't fall out. This can mean that there is no right or wrong, no good or bad only different views.

The Christian position is very different from the current society around us. We believe that a creator God who in love made the universe and everything in it including humanity and made it very good; that humanity given free choice was seduced by pride and turned against God. This cataclysmic rebellion

Of man's first disobedience and the fruit
Of that forbidden tree, whose mortal taste
Brought death into the world and all our woe
With loss of Eden...[5]

resulted in a world which causes not just all humanity much sadness, but God also. There are absolutes. There is good and bad; there is truth and falsehood. We believe that this 'fall' is so great and complete that we are not able

---

[4]   More commonly, "If I have the power I take your money and give it to those I consider less privileged than you. In this way I can feel self satisfied at no cost to myself".

[5]   John Milton's Paradise Lost lines 1-4

to save ourselves in spite of every effort. We need to be rescued. This is where Jesus Christ comes in -

> *...till one greater man*
> *Restore us and regain the blissful seat.*[6]

Our Christian teaching and experience leads us to conclude that both God and humanity are dissatisfied with a broken world and the most wonderful news is that God Himself has faced up to the problem and come into the world to show humanity that it can be fixed. This means that there is a role for us and God has not sidelined us but wants us together with Him to work out His purposes. This gives us a choice. We can go our own way and ignore God, which is the way of secularist societies, or we can cooperate with Him. The purpose of this book is to assert that Britain at various times in her history did just this.

It seems that in a free society there needs to be a 'critical mass' of like minded people to effect a change of direction in a community or nation. Significant numbers of Christian people have existed in Britain from time to time and have influenced important changes in many facets of life. When this 'critical mass' of Christians is present things happen, progress is made and individuals and society flourish. When it is absent the nation stagnates and loses direction and purpose. It is the claim of this book that godly principles and godly people have produced an outpouring of ideas and activities beneficial to all humanity.

---

[6] Paradise Lost lines 4-5

In no way is there a claim Christian men and women are in any way superior to those who don't subscribe to this faith. Our only claim is that we have found where we can receive spiritual forgiveness and nurturing which brings us in touch, in a mysterious way, with the creator and sustainer of our world who seems willing to come alongside us and give us His benefits. And these benefits are significant such as life, fulfillment, His very self and resurrection from the dead! There is hope for a future that no other belief system can match. This means that God can inspire ordinary people to address seemingly insurmountable problems not looking to human resources or responding to all too common human discouragement. He can inspire people to think new thoughts, break new ground and do things never done before. This is illustrated by the fact that Christian northern Europe (especially Britain) and north America have produced more beneficial inventions than anywhere else in the world.

When God is included it means that a Christian environment or framework can enable ordinary activities which are morally neutral and not overtly Christian to germinate in a way impossible in a purely materialistic secular climate.

It needs to be pointed out however, that even when we choose to cooperate with God we always bring our imperfect humanity with us and this results in imperfect ideas, plans and actions. So even our best is tainted.

An example of how a non materialistic and morally significant approach to events has occurred in the past is

Aleksander Solzhenitsyn's remarks in a BBC interview in 1976 when he said;

I am surprised that pragmatic philosophy consistently scorns moral considerations - and nowadays in the Western press we read a candid declaration of the principle that moral considerations have nothing to do with politics. They do not apply, and should not, so to speak, be applied. I would remind you that in 1939 England thought differently. If moral considerations were not applicable to politics, then it would have been quite incomprehensible why on earth England went to war with Hitler's Germany. Pragmatically, you could have got out of the situation. But England chose the moral course and experienced and demonstrated to the world perhaps the most brilliant and heroic period in its history.[7]

Another point that needs to be made is that the intellectual climate dominating early twenty first century Britain is formed by aggressive materialistic humanism which has no place for God. This is dangerous as it leaves a moral vacuum which is filled by various undesirable ideologies which are destructive to our hard won liberties.

Arrogant pride in the human mind coupled with fear of Islamic extremism has brought to the surface fervent anti Christian outbursts – Christians being a safe target, as any explicit criticism of Islam runs the risk of a violent response. This anti Christian bias has been festering for a long time, coming into the open in the last half century having been made respectable by mainly socialist

---

[7]   Aleksander Solzhenitsyn in a BBC interview 1976 reported in the Times Tues 05Aug08

thinkers. In a perverse way this has given rise to the denigration of all British accomplishments. The thinking has gone like this. If Britain has contributed so much to the world there must be a reason. Something has made the British able to produce and accomplish so much. The only logical answers are, an outside inspiring force such as God or the British are a superior people. Racial superiority is rightly discarded and as in the minds of our leaders God does not exist he too must be discarded. There is therefore no answer, so the question must also be discarded. Thus from the last half of the twentieth century a society which has no place for God also has no place for Britain able to take a realistic view of its own history and accomplishments.

Very few people are deliberately evil. Most of us have high ideals, desires and principles, but often do not meet our own standards and more often fail to meet other people's standards for us. Hypocrisy is a common human vice - one we can all relate to and what is true of individuals is also true of nations.

Coming from a Christian position in the midst of a secular humanistic society it is necessary to state as clearly as possible the guiding principles behind the statement that Britain is the most successful nation in the history of the world.

This book is a shameless celebration of Britain; of individuals – thinkers, explorers, rulers, missionaries, fighting men, lawyers and politicians; of institutions; of ideas and inventions. It is also a recognition that Britain, like all nations is made up of individuals; and nations just as individuals are capable of bad as well as good. There is much which is not commendable in British history just as there is in the lives of individuals, but the good heavily outweighs the bad.

This book starts by stating the imperfectability of humanity. Untold effort cannot raise a man. Only God can do it. The twentieth century has proved with its numberless wars and destructive ideologies that the idea that humanity is evolving within the framework of universal education and benign state guidance towards a position superior to our ancestors is a lie. We cannot pull ourselves up by our bootstraps. We need rescuing from our own universal depravity; we cannot save ourselves. Our acknowledgement of our need and our acceptance of what God offers in Jesus Christ opens doors for unimaginable blessings. It also cannot be emphasized too forcefully that no nation or individual is superior to any other, '*for all have sinned and fallen short of the glory of God*[8].

Every facet of the national life of Britain is saturated with the Christian faith.

---

[8]   The Bible - Letter to the Romans chap 3 verse 23

Chapter 2

WHERE'S THE COMPETITION?

It is the claim that the most successful nation in the history of the world is Britain. Not the richest; not the biggest, not the most powerful. There are other contenders. This claim needs to be examined by considering other possible contenders.

ANCIENT GREECE and ROME

These two ancient and long lasting empires do not qualify as their societies were always based on slavery.

USA

The USA is the most prominent competitor, but it is disqualified for just one reason. It was made in England; it has an English foundation. The United States is a super power and of all the New World nations by far the most successful. It wins first prize in many areas but not this one. The America we know was founded in the early

1600s, less than 400 years ago. Virginia and New England were English plantations. They were setup by English people who brought with them English law, government and customs, but most of all they brought with them the Christian faith. They quickly grew, established the rule of law, direct democracy and a love of liberty which resulted in their independence from the mother country 150 years after their founding. Even after this time, right up to the second world war, the USA lived as an often unruly offspring in the shadow of its parent. Much of its current greatness is not of its own making but inherited from Britain.

The territorial dimensions of the USA were established by Britain in the wars of the mid 18th century where France and Holland were excluded from the north American eastern seaboard. Spain was also sidelined, so when the 13 colonies gained their independence there was no other foreign power able to prevent their expansion. Britain gained control of the seas in the French revolutionary and Napoleonic wars and all other maritime powers were excluded from North America. This exclusion forced France to sell her remaining territory to the new United States in the Louisiana Purchase, thus opening up the route to the Pacific ocean and the establishment of the present boundaries.

FRANCE

Ah! La Belle France. In many ways France should be the most successful nation. She is blessed with some of the best geography; both temperate and Mediterranean climates; fine rivers, natural harbours, majestic mountains;

fertile and productive land – all of it world famous. Her people are among the most creative on earth – French artists in all spheres, philosophers, engineers (French engineers invented the screw[9]), architects, ship builders, soldiers, etc. And yet there was a flaw. The 16th century St. Bartholomew's day massacre of thousands of French subjects for their religious views was a blot on the country when surviving Huguenots, many with great skills, fled the country. Thousands came to England in both the 17th and 18th centuries giving Britain and other countries an advantage at France's expense.

Again in the revolutionary and Napoleonic wars lasting from 1789 to 1815 (with very short breaks) caused the deaths of countless French people for what were ideological reasons. It is said that when the Chinese communist dictator Mao Tse Tung was asked what had been the consequences of the French Revolution, he replied that it was too early to tell, implying that France has still not recovered from the barbarism of organised mass slaughter. The lack of a recognisable and acknowledged Godly dimension to French national life has left the nation diminished in a rather sad way.

GERMANY

Germany led the world in Christian spirituality at the time of the reformation; their thinkers, bible scholars and leaders inspired and challenged the rest of Europe. At about this time Johannes Gutenberg perfected the removable type press which allowed the explosion of

---

[9] Actually they invented the metal screw. The Romans and Greeks invented wooden screws.

information throughout Europe. Germany led the way in many fields, but a centralised state which crushed individual thinking coupled with Godless philosophy provided a fertile ground for the growth of deadly ideas which eventually gave rise to Nazism. The result was a world war and mass murder on an incomprehensible scale from which not only Germany, but all the world, is still recovering. It is sobering to know that not even the most cultured and civilised nations are immune from deadly diabolical influences.

ITALY

Italy never stood a chance. Though the birthplace of the renaissance it was held in the vice like grip of tyranny. The Roman Catholic Church was the dominant political and cultural force of the day controlling all facets of society, even thought and belief. The intellectual establishment was of such arrogance that it stifled all genuine enquiry which did not fit its preconceptions. They were like the 'alchemists' of every generation who only accept as truth that which supports their pet theories, irrespective of where the evidence leads. The treatment of Galileo is the world's most famous example of blinkered pseudo-science attempting to crush the truth. He challenged the ancient earth-centered Ptolemaic and Aristotelian theories of astronomy which were accepted by the scientific establishment of the day and supported the sun-centered Copernican theory of the universe which asserted that the earth and the planets orbited the sun. The scientific powers of the day forced him to make a public recantation of his views and placed him under house arrest for the rest of his life. The Italian genius instead of being nurtured and built up was restricted, ground down and stunted.

RUSSIA

Being a nation in the middle of the largest land mass on earth, Russia seems to have the thinking that it must always expand or it is bound to contract. It bullied its neighbours, as all strong nations are prone to do, expanding eastwards to include the Central Asian Muslim states reaching to China, northwards absorbing the Siberian wilderness, westwards conquering ancient nations such as Lithuania, Georgia and Ukraine. It reached its maximum size as the Soviet Union. The deliberate Godlessness of the communist government resulted in the misery and death of untold millions of citizens of that state. No contest.

Stalin wrote, "One feature of the history of old Russia was the continual beatings she suffered because of her backwardness. She was beaten by the Turkish Beys. She was beaten by the Swedish feudal lords. She was beaten by the Polish and Lithuanian gentry. She was beaten by the British and French capitalists. She was beaten by the Japanese barons. All beat her because of her backwardness[10]...." It was this distorted sense of inferiority which drove Russia and to destroy her own people and to attack and seek to subjugate nearby states. This could be the same fear which makes Stalin's successors behave so aggressively towards their neighbours.

---

[10] Piers Brendon – The Dark Valley p208. J Haslam – Soviet foreign policy 1930-33

SPAIN

One of the first modern nations Spain was in a very privileged position. She had a disciplined and gifted population and quickly monopolised the Americas, concentrating on the extraordinarily rich central and South American nations which provided gold and silver in such abundance. Vast wealth so easily obtained, coupled with a centralised overbearing government distorted and corrupted the nation. Spain like Italy, dominated by an unreformed Roman Catholic Church, never attained its full potential.

CHINA and JAPAN

It is almost an impertinence to lump these two countries together. However, both were relatively late in joining the modern world, both deliberately shutting themselves off.

In the early 1400s the Chinese built and maintained large fleets of big ocean going ships capable of crossing the Pacific Ocean. These were far larger and more sophisticated than the ships the Portuguese explorers had[11]. The blinkered, self satisfied and insular Chinese rulers turned against exploration and foreign trade insisting that China did not need anything foreign. So at the end of the century anyone who built a ship with more than two masts was liable to the death penalty. Similarly up to 1853 it was a capital offence for anyone in Japan to build ocean going ships.

---

[11] P96 Wealth and poverty of nations – When China ruled the seas by Louise Levathes

Both the Chinese and Japanese emperors believed that they were descended from a sun god and were leaders of nations destined to bring light and civilisation to the world[12]. Their modern successors inspired in one case by the brutality of depraved philosophy and in the other of a sense of racial superiority caused untold misery to their own people and the world at large.

The rest of the world

Africa, South America, the Middle East and many nations of Europe and Asia do not appear in this list.

Most of Sub Saharan Africa only climbed out of savagery with the arrival of the colonial powers, who first exploited them for slaves, before bringing a sense of law and order.

The South American nations, the offspring of Spain and Portugal, were initially settled by adventurers, soldiers and exploiters who were less keen to build nations than to enrich themselves. The foundation of these nations gave them a serious disadvantage from which they have still not recovered.

The Middle East and the North African states being mainly Muslim suffer from a religion which does not encourage freedom of thought. So these gifted people have not achieved their promise.

* * *

---

[12] P335 Wealth and poverty of nations & chap 9 The dark valley

Looking at the history of all nations it seems that human nature has an affinity for totalitarian and absolute government; that those who wield power seek to retain it at what ever cost. And Lord Acton's words written in1887 that *"Power tends to corrupt, and absolute power corrupts absolutely.."* has struck a chord everywhere.

The idea takes root that government always knows best and democracies are only partially protected from this presumption. Voters in free countries have a choice and can and do kick out a governing party. An election can see a visible change of government, but underneath there is the same root. A permanent civil service does not easily change and if it is dominated by Godless people seduced by corrupt ideologies, the outlook is not bright.

At the beginning of the twenty first century Britain can still claim to be the most successful nation in the history of the world, but if current trends continue she will lose this position sooner or later. Up to the end of the second world war Britain was a major world power in every sense of the term. So the title of most successful nation was a reality. Britain's decline since then makes the title historical, but the legacy is still stupendous.

Chapter 3

A PEARL WITHOUT PRICE

For most of the last two thousand years Christianity has had an impact on life in Britain; Christian Roman soldiers; Celtic missionaries, early Roman Catholics through to the corrupted church of the late middle ages, to the flowering at the reformation. Right up to recent times God has been recognised with varying degrees of clarity and acceptance. It is only in the twentieth century that humanity has been seduced by destructive godless ideologies which have resulted in the slaughter of countless millions all over the world. Britain has been anchored in the Christian faith and the Bible has always been a forceful influence, particularly since the sixteenth century. The first translations of the Bible into English was done by John Wycliffe in the 1380s and distributed by his followers the Lollards. However, it took more than two hundred years for the Bible in English to be reliably available.

Two passages serve to illustrate how scripture has infiltrated the personal life of individuals and the corporate life of the political nation. These are;

Love must be sincere. Hate what is evil; cling to what is good. Be devoted to one another in brotherly love. Honour one another above yourselves. Never be lacking in zeal, but keep your spiritual fervour, serving the Lord. Be joyful in hope, patient in affliction, faithful in prayer. Share with God's people who are in need. Practice hospitality. Bless those who persecute you; bless and do not curse. Rejoice with those who rejoice; mourn with those who mourn. Live in harmony with one another. Do not be proud, but be willing to associate with people of low position. Do not be conceited.

Do not repay anyone evil for evil. Be careful to do what is right in the eyes of everybody. If it is possible, as far as it depends on you, live at peace with everyone. Do not take revenge, my friends, but leave room for God's wrath, for it is written; "It is mine to avenge; I will repay," says the Lord. On the contrary:

"If your enemy is hungry, feed him;
If he is thirsty, give him something to drink.
In doing this, you will heap burning coals on his head."
Do not be overcome by evil, but overcome evil with good.[13]

This passage is one of many which spell out the importance of personal behaviour and the fundamental requirement for love and forgiveness in all human relationships. Feeding your enemy, living humbly and not taking revenge are all contrary to human nature,

---

[13] The Bible – Letter to the Romans chap 12 from verse 9

but these words have entered into the lives of countless people all over the world and especially in Britain. It is Bible passages like the above which have been the main cause why for centuries there has been social cohesion and stability in spite of cruel gaps between rich and poor. It is also the reason why Britain has been surprisingly free from the family and social feuding which has scarred so many other countries.

Jesus said:

The kings of the gentiles lord it over them; and those who exercise authority over them call themselves Benefactors. But you are not to be like that. Instead, the greatest among you should be like the youngest, and the one who rules like the one who serves[14].

This passage has been a touchstone for all leaders in all walks of life. Even in politics the leader and his advisers are called ministers, implying that they render aid to or supply the needs of others. Again this is contrary to human nature as Jesus said, the rulers of the gentiles lord it over them. In many nations the rulers have the power of life and death over their people – even to this day. In England the influence, not only of the Bible, but the direct inspiration of God's Holy Spirit in the lives of his people has seeped into the life of the nation and has had an impact for good which needs to be acknowledged and acclaimed.

The claim that Britain is the most successful nation in the history of the world rests on a broad foundation.

---

[14] The Bible – Lukes Gospel chap 22 from verse 25

One of the most significant cornerstones is the English constitution[15].

In ancient times leaders who were challenged simply killed their opponents, if they could; it was a case of "either him or me". (This principle still applies in many nations even now.) In England the hereditary monarchy allowed a seamless transfer of power from one generation to the next as institutions were slowly setup which acted in the king's name but did not need the king to be present; such as when the inheritor of the throne was an infant. This is what happened when king John died in 1216 and whose eldest son, Henry III, was nine years old. Until Henry came of age the country was run by a Council of Regency and it was during the thirteenth century that the foundation was laid for Parliament and the justice system to be taken out of the king's control. These two trends matured to eventually impose national fetters on the exercise of the personal will of the monarch.

The king allowing judges to decide cases not according to his own personal opinions, but according to the laws and customs of the realm, was really allowing them to act in his name according to the wishes of his subjects.

The early Parliaments in the reign of Henry's son king Edward I, were called for the purpose of granting money for the king's needs - mainly wars with Wales, Scotland and France. The representatives came from the counties and larger towns and were summoned to come with 'full and sufficient powers from their communities'. This

---

[15]   Much in this chapter relies on 'The government of the British Empire' by E. Jenks

meant that no questions could be raised as to the limits of the powers of the English Parliament. In spite of civil war and the opposition of ruthless kings, these institutions grew in influence and importance, Parliament growing more conscious of its powers came to demand 'redress of grievances' before granting supply and eventually becoming a stern critic of the king's government.

It is noteworthy to observe that continental Diets, States-General and Parliaments also existed about this time, but none had the same potential of the English Parliament and were emasculated by overbearing tyrannical kings.

With the reformation coming to England and then the publication of the Authorised Version of the Bible in 1611 the impact of the Christian gospel on all walks of life was immense. The political struggles in the first half of the seventeenth century had a significant religious dimension; the English civil war was remarkable in that devoted Christians fought on both sides at all levels from the humblest to highest. The letter from William Waller to his friend Ralph Hopton is a moving account of close affection of men on opposing sides[16]. Oliver

---

[16] "Certainly my affections to you are so unchangeable, that hostility itself cannot violate my friendship to your person, but I must be true to the cause wherein I serve… I should most gladly wait on you according to your desire, but that I look upon you as you are engaged in that party, beyond a possibility of retreat …And I know the conference would never be so close (ie secret) between us, but that it would take wind and receive a construction to my dishonour. That great God who is the searcher of my heart knows with what a sad sense I go upon this service, and with what a perfect hatred I detest this war without an enemy; but I look upon it as sent from God and that is enough to silence all passion in me. The God of peace in his own time send us peace,

Cromwell was the most famous leader who took his faith very seriously. The civil war was brutal and caused vast suffering throughout Britain and Ireland. Victory for the Parliamentary forces was followed by 12 years of various forms of government under Cromwell. There were several experiments in how best to rule the three kingdoms of England, Scotland and Ireland, but none proved to be sustainable or acceptable. The monarchy was restored shortly after Cromwell's death, but many valuable lessons had been learnt. Also there was no mass retributive killing in Britain by the victorious sides which meant that at the restoration the healing of the nation was remarkable.

It was during the century and a half following the English civil war that legal status was given to various provisions which protect the citizen from the arbitrary power of the state.

HABEAS CORPUS

Habeas Corpus, also known as 'the great writ', was anchored in law to protect citizens from arbitrary arrest and imprisonment. The right to petition for a writ of habeas corpus has long been celebrated as the most efficient safeguard of the liberty of the subject.

---

and in the mean time fit us to receive it: we are both upon the stage and must act such parts as are assigned us in this tragedy. Let us do it in a way of Honour and without personal animosities whatsoever the issue be, I shall never willingly relinquish the dear title of your most affectionate and faithful servant"
From Waller's letter to Sir Ralph Hopton, 16th June 1643

This famous writ was originally a document issued in an ordinary prosecution bidding the sheriff to 'have the body' of the defendant in prison ready for the trial of the case. Now, if the jailer who obeys the writ can show good cause for the imprisonment the order for the writ is not made 'absolute' and the prisoner stays in prison. The writ was freely used in the contest between King Charles I and his parliaments. One of the first acts of the Long Parliament in 1640 was to pass a statute guaranteeing the right to the writ of Habeas Corpus in all cases, to all persons imprisoned on whatever grounds and was reinforced by the more famous Act of 1679. Habeas Corpus safeguards the citizen from arbitrary arrest and imprisonment.

Albert Venn Dicey, the famous Victorian constitutional jurist, wrote that the Habeas Corpus Acts "declare no principle and define no rights, but they are for practical purposes worth a hundred constitutional articles guaranteeing individual liberty."

INDEPENDENCE of JUDICIARY

As already noted, from the thirteenth century the king took no personal part in the proceedings of his law courts so the personal whim of the king had to be subject to the law. No English king could claim "The state is me". However, up to the end of the seventeenth century judges were appointed by the king 'during his pleasure'; that is they could be dismissed at any moment for any or no reason. As a result of the Act of Settlement of the year 1700 judges were appointed for life and cannot be dismissed except for an actual crime. Also by the same Act judges income was made independent of royal favour. In time this came to guarantee British judges independence from the government of the day, their impartiality and uprightness.

SEPARATION of POWERS

If the three arms of the state, the executive, the legislature and the judiciary, are held by one body such as the king, a president or a party then this is a totalitarian government giving rise to dictatorship and tyranny. The worst cases of this have been seen in the twentieth century with National Socialism (Nazi) in Germany and International Socialism (Communism) in the Soviet Union, China, etc. This is bad government bringing misery, poverty and death to countless millions of people.

In England as has been noted the judges were independent of the ruler from early times which constrained the king and after many centuries developed an enviable independence and impartiality.

In England the group of leaders known as the Cabinet are chosen from the dominant party in Parliament and it is the Cabinet which has executive power in the nation. It is the Cabinet - that is the governing party - which determines the legislative program and dominates Parliament. This close link, where the executive controls the legislature, runs the risk of despotism or an 'elective dictatorship' which Lord Hailsham warned about in the 1960s. It is only in recent years that this risk has become a reality with Members of Parliament serving their party rather than their constituents. Hasty often ill conceived laws have been passed without the rigorous debate and discussion which is always necessary. In earlier Parliaments men and women of character and judgement have been elected and these have had an independent quality which has been able to hold governments to account.

FREEDOM of EXPRESSION

Every free society guarantees freedom of speech and expression. But in many cases the guarantees given by the state, usually wrapped up in fine constitutional rhetoric, have often been tragically meaningless.

In England free expression has not been a privilege given by a government to the people. Ordinary people have struggled to acquire and retain it. It is claimed that this freedom goes back into the mists of time. An Englishman can claim to be born with freedom of speech which no Act of Parliament can remove. Magna Carta enshrines general liberties in law which any government interferes with at their peril.

John Milton wrote in 'Areopagitica[17]' his appeal to freedom of expression,

"Give me the liberty to know, to utter, and to argue freely according to conscience, above all liberties'.

His was a commitment to truth and the need for freedom to utter it, made at a time when the state licensed all publishing. His writings contributed to this freedom in England, such as the famous quote also from 'Areopagitica',

"Though all the winds of doctrine were let loose to play upon the earth, so Truth be in the field, we do injuriously by licensing and prohibiting to misdoubt her strength. Let her and falsehood grapple; who ever knew Truth put to the worse, in a free and open encounter?"

The Christian approach to free expression is to welcome it with open arms. It means of course that foolish and even bad ideas will be expressed, but let Truth and falsehood grapple in free and open debate and the outcome is not in doubt.

RULE of LAW

The Rule of Law lays down the principle, that no act of any official, even the highest, however, bona fide and apparently reasonable, which infringes the liberty or rights of a citizen, is justifiable, unless it is authorised by law. For any such unlawful act, by whatever authority commanded, the official is personally liable in an action

---

[17]   Might best be translated as 'marketplace for ideas'

in the ordinary court. This principle rightly puts a real constraint on the zeal of interfering officials.

* * *

It may be claimed that Britain has the finest constitutional settlement the world has ever seen. It has worked well for over 300 years in good times and in bad.

It may be informative to consider what bad times really mean. Let us take 1797 as an example – over 200 years ago – it was an interesting year. Britain had had stable good government for over a century. There was the rule of law, fairly open government, liberty of the people and bloodless transfer of power.

In 1797 though, things were pretty bad. Firstly, the country was losing a major war. All our allies had deserted us and many people were clamouring for peace. Our enemy, although negotiating was not serious, only wishing to extract as much advantage as possible. Secondly, inflation was bad; the national finances were in a bad way. Thirdly, the harvest had been poor and food was scarce and expensive; many poorer people were going hungry.

If that were not enough, there was a run on the Bank of England. The notes saying, "I promise to pay the bearer on demand…" were being handed in and real money demanded. Only gold would do! There was not enough bullion to guarantee the paper. Added to this several provincial banks became bankrupt.

To cap it all the Royal Navy, which as the only thing which protected the country from invasion had mutinied. The Channel fleet and the North Sea fleet refused to obey orders. Also the army was considered unreliable.

The constitution was strained, but did not break. This was because it was not an abstract ideal, but something created, developed and nurtured by free men and women who took their liberties seriously. The freedom of the people was not destroyed; the rule of law was intact and ultimately the constitution was strengthened. 1797 was a bad year. Britain has had other bad years since then as well as good, but the constitution has stood the test of time in good and bad and has served the country well. Looking at the history of most other nations it is noteworthy they have not fared as well.

There has been a significant Christian framework surrounding British constitutional activity for many centuries and although there have been perhaps only a few Christian men and women active in public life they have had a significant impact on standards. The truths in the bible have permeated their lives and the framework within which they worked and the following instructions of a Jewish king to his judges is an example of why there has been high standards; "*Consider carefully what you do, because you are not judging for man but for the LORD, who is with you whenever you give a verdict. Now let the fear of the LORD be upon you. Judge carefully, for with the LORD our God there is no injustice or partiality or bribery.[18]*"

---

[18]   The bible – 2 Chronicles chap 19 v 6,7

English, and more recently British, constitutional development has been a haphazard and sometimes bloody affair over many centuries. However, since the acts of settlement in the late seventeenth century it has meant that for more than three hundred years England has been able to change her government without bloodshed.

That indeed is a pearl without price unmatched by any other nation.

Chapter 4

PAX BRITANNICA

God of our fathers, known of old--
Lord of our far-flung battle line
Beneath whose awful hand we hold
Dominion over palm and pine--
Lord God of Hosts, be with us yet,

Far-called, our navies melt away;
On dune and headland sinks the fire:
Lo, all our pomp of yesterday
Is one with Nineveh and Tyre!
Judge of the Nations, spare us yet,
Lest we forget - lest we forget![19]

"The empire made Britain great. Without it, as its statesmen and service chiefs privately reiterated, the mother country would be an insignificant island anchored forlornly off the coast of Europe".[20]   So wrote Piers

---

[19] Rudyard Kipling's - Recessional

[20] Piers Brendon – The Dark Valley p 372

Brendon about Britain and its diffident and appeasing leaders in the late 1930s. This insignificant forlorn island which had been the world's policeman for well over a century and would be for another 40 years, had lately fought a world war which cost something like 2.6 million casualties of her brightest and best (more than 10 times that of the USA) and was enduring the world recession which would only end with yet another world war.

Empires have had their day. Unlike two centuries ago, today there are few unknown, backward tribal people. Even as late as the 1895 the Times Atlas unapologetically showed large parts of Africa and Asia as blank – unexplored, unknown areas. Now there are none.

So how was it that this disparaged nation came to acquire the largest and farthest flung empire the world has even seen, how it not only acquired it, but held and developed it, how it planted daughter nations which are today the envy of the world and how it inspired loyalty and support in many wars including two world wars? The answers are many and various.

Firstly, the British are an aggressive people; whenever there is a scrap or punch up they like to be involved. But then, so are many other nations, French, Spanish, German, Japanese, Russians, Chinese etc. Secondly, Britain for over 200 years controlled the seas. The Royal Navy sailed wherever it wished and could prevent others if it desired. Thirdly, after the unsought American war of independence, Britain learnt how to manage her colonies. And by the end of the eighteenth century the moral climate in Britain was changing, mainly because of the preaching of the Christian gospel by the Wesley brothers and others which meant that people serving overseas, especially in India, were not as grasping and selfish as earlier. From this time the concept of service and self giving grew up.

The experience of Britain in India deserves looking at in some detail, because it was the richest and in some ways the most important of the countries in the empire. It was a relationship which plumbed the depths of brutality but also laid the foundations for modern India and gave much to the country.

England's relationship with India began when the East India Company was setup by royal warrant as one of the last acts of Queen Elizabeth on 31st December 1600. It took decades for the English merchants to be accepted in the court of the Mogul emperors but over the next hundred years Britain was able to set up trading stations in Bengal, Madras and Bombay. However, in the eighteenth century Britain and France exported their rivalry to all parts of the world and in India the princes and rulers who were allies of the French automatically became Britain's enemies and of course wars resulted. On the outbreak of the Seven Years' war (1756-1763) the French government, determined to drive the British out of India, sent a powerful land and naval force. It arrived too late. The battle of Plassey had been won by Clive and the French being deserted by their local allies were expelled from India never to return as a political force. In conflict with the local Indian rulers the East India Company, which was in India to trade, quickly found itself responsible for governing large areas of Bengal. Unfortunately this responsibility was only partial as the company had real power, but was nominally accountable to the local rulers. This form of dual government led to serious abuses which were not resolved until the end of the century. Warren Hastings was appointed Governor in 1772 and he is credited with stamping out trading abuses by the Company's servants who were thereafter given adequate salaries which meant there was no need for them to trade fraudulently. Hastings also introduced a regular system of protection in Bengal. He set up border police who drove the Himalayan bandits from the country and wiped out the gangs of armed robbers who plagued the region.

Lord Cornwallis (appointed in 1786) and his successor Lord Wellesley (appointed in 1798) reformed the revenue administration in Bengal and oversaw the expansion of British territory.

The coming of the nineteenth century saw the British established as one of the main ruling powers in India and had acquired Ceylon which was taken from the Dutch who had been conquered by France in the revolutionary wars. It is in the next 150 years and especially in the half century up to the Indian Mutiny that there was a constant commitment to India by hundreds of men and women from every walk of life who in many cases spent their whole lives in a country which was most unhealthy for Europeans. They were soldiers, administrators, doctors, nurses, missionaries, explorers and others and much good was done for the government, prosperity and safety of India. There follows sketches of four individuals who made a significant impact on the life of the country.

CHARLES METCALFE[21]

Charles Metcalfe landed at Calcutta on 1st January 1801 not quite 16 years old. He was apprenticed to various political officers and in 1808 at the age of 23 he was made Envoy to Ranjit Singh the ruler of the Punjab. Ranjit Singh was a man of immense courage, perseverance and political wisdom who established and consolidated the Sikh kingdom ruled from Lahore. "Against this hard-riding, hard-drinking, lustful, shrewd barbarian was pitted young Charles from Eton, a complex, introspective creature who kept a diary and noted in it thoughts on self-love and duty, sin and suffering." Metcalfe's mission to Lahore was to persuade Ranjit Singh to enter into some sort of alliance with Britain against Napoleon. He was unsuccessful but established a good relationship with the Punjab and the Sikhs were reasonably friendly with Britain and did not attack India territory east of the river Sutlej until after Ranjit Singh's death.

In 1812 at the age of 27 Metcalfe was appointed Resident at Delhi to the court of the Mogul emperor. The Resident was in theory a diplomat, but Metcalfe was in fact an administrator of an area the size of Wales. The Delhi administration under his rule was the most enlightened in the world. He abolished capital punishment and flogging and forbade the slave trade and the burning of widows.

After 8 years in Delhi he went first to Calcutta then to Hyderabad where he fought corruption and cleaned up

---

[21] These individuals deserve and have full biographies themselves. This brief sketch is from Philip Mason 'The men who ruled India'.

the administration. He did not go back to England for 37 years and eventually held the post of Governor General for two years during which time he passed a measure freeing the English written press from censorship. A man of faith he wrote, "*I live in a state of fervent and incessant gratitude to God for the favours and mercies which I have experienced. The feeling is so strong that it often overflows in tears and is so rooted that I do not think any misfortunes could shake it*".

Metcalfe in common with many other Britons in India at this time and later was aware that Britain had a guardian role only in the country and concerning British presence in India he wrote, "*Our dominion in India is by conquest; it is naturally disgusting to the inhabitants and can only be maintained by military force. It is our positive duty to render them justice, to respect and protect their rights, and to study their happiness. By the performance of this duty, we may allay and keep dormant their innate disaffection; but the expectation of purchasing their cordial attachment by gratuitous alienations of public revenue would be a vain delusion*".

WILLIAM SLEEMAN

Possibly one of the most horrifying books ever written is 'The confessions of a Thug' by Philip Meadows Taylor. It is a continuous tale of the premeditated murder of innocent, unsuspecting travellers in all parts of India by the Thugs. These men, almost bred to murder, operated in gangs who charmed themselves into the company of nervous travellers and in remote places along the road strangled, robbed and buried them with amazing speed in a ritualistic way. It was a demonic as well as a gruesome business as it was not just a crime for gain. Killing was the first object as this secret society believed they had been entrusted by the vile goddess Kali with the duty of murdering travellers. The highways and waterways of India had been unsafe for generations where tens of thousands[22] disappeared without trace; and the Thugs were the reason.

A Cornishman, William Sleeman had been in India 20 years and was working as a political officer in central India when he heard about the activities of the Thugs. A Thug murder attempt on a group of native Indian soldiers known as sepoys misfired, the gang was captured and a few members became informers, known as approvers. Sleeman meticulously interrogated them and laboriously compiled a comprehensive indictment which resulted in the gang being tried, found guilty and sentenced, some to death others to imprisonment. It was known that Thugs operated throughout the continent and Sleeman understood that the evidence taken from approvers was packed with clues which could lead him to other gangs. In the 1830s Sleeman, helped by about only twenty young officers, built up a list of members of each gang and the crimes they had committed over the previous fifteen or so years. The evidence had to be impeccable as any discrepancy would be taken as a sign of innocence. "The judges must have clear, corroborated, uncontradicted testimony, because they stood for the rule of law as

---

[22] It is estimated that between 20,000 and 40,000 people were killed each year

against the individual whim that had ruled before."[23]   In these few years forty or fifty gangs were destroyed and more than three thousand Thugs were convicted. Thus a small band of dedicated men working methodically and with a purpose was able to wipe out a despicable evil and stamp out Thugs and hopefully the craft is forgotten.

SIR GEORGE EVEREST and others

Cape Comorin is the most southerly point of the Indian mainland. By the time he retired in 1843 George Everest, the Surveyor General of India and Superintendent of the Great Trigonometrical Survey, had supervised the largest survey on earth from Cape Comorin to the foothills of the Himalayas - a distance of almost 1500 miles.

It was started in 1806 in the middle of a world war by Everest's predecessor William Lambton who was a master of precision. Between 1803 and 1805 Lambton surveyed across the Indian peninsular from Madras in the East to Mangalore on the West coast. Starting from each end of a precisely measured seven and half mile baseline at Madras he and his small team calculated the angles of a series of triangles[24] whose sides were measured in miles, sometime up to forty. The precise dimensions of the triangles were calculated and a series of points were established across the continent. At the half way point Lambton checked his calculations by doing a ground

---

[23]   Philip Mason 'The men who ruled India'.

[24]   Given the two angles from each end of the baseline to a fixed point at a distance and using trigonometry it is possible to calculate the distance of the fixed point from each end of the base line thus providing a new base line for further triangles.

measurement of a new baseline against that which had been predetermined by trigonometry. This new base line was over 7 miles long and two hundred miles from Madras. The difference between the ground measured length and the trigonometric calculated length was just 3.7 inches. This was an extraordinary testimony to the accuracy of Lambton's precise measurements and mathematical calculations. It was also a recognition of the quality of his equipment, especially of his theodolite. This carefully calibrated precision instrument weighing half a ton was carried across some of the most difficult terrain and hauled to the top of hills, towers and sometimes temples. There were only two or three theodolites of the required accuracy in the world and one was acquired from England.

Lambton now commenced the 'Great Arc' working north from Cape Comorin and he instructed his assistant George Everest to conduct a secondary survey west from Hyderabad to towards Bombay. These surveys across very difficult country where malarial jungle and unfriendly natives added to the tedious backbreaking work of clearing line of sight paths and rendered progress very slow. The need to wait for clear weather to allow correct sightings also added to the time taken. Sickness often laid men low and Everest had to take leave at Capetown to convalesce. This survey took a long time and it was in 1823 that Lambton died suddenly near Nagpur in central India. Everest was now appointed as the senior surveyor in India and over the next twenty years he continued the survey of the 'Great Arc' up to the foothills of the Himalayas.

Lambton, Everest and their assistants were persevering dedicated men who did not let any difficulty interfere with their ambition, neither did they compromise on the quality of their measurements and calculations. Everest retired to England in 1843 and it is not known whether or not he ever laid his eyes on the great mountain that bears his name, but his triangulation network was extended and used to locate the summit by Andrew Waugh, his successor as Surveyor General in India. Waugh's admiration of Everest's achievements led to the naming of "Peak XV" in the Himalayas. After its discovery by his team, Waugh, wrote: "...here is a mountain most probably the highest in the world without any local name that I can discover...", so he proposed "...to perpetuate the memory of that illustrious master of geographical research...Everest."

SIR BARTLE FRERE

"Bombay has a lower death rate in the last two years than London, the healthiest city in Europe. This is entirely your doing. If we do not take care, Bombay will outstrip us in the sanitary race. People will be ordered for the benefit of their health to Bombay". So wrote Florence Nightingale to Sir Bartle Frere in 1869. Public works were his interest as was improving the education of Indians, especially girls as female education was neglected in India at that time. In the middle years of the century he worked tirelessly to improve the infrastructure of the Sind province and Bombay. Irrigation, roads, railways, land reclamation as well as public works such as municipal buildings, clean water supply and public sanitation are his legacy. As Governor of the Bombay Presidency he took Bombay from a disease ridden backwater to a world class city. Bartle Frere was a man of vision who used his position to bring about improvements which brought benefits to countless people. Much of his time was spent in conflict with smaller bureaucratic minds in the higher reaches of the central Imperial government, which at that time was in Calcutta. India has benefited from his perseverance, commitment and faith that there is more to governing than politics and finance.

Sir Bartle Frere believed that the British rule in India was for the benefit of the people of India and it was to be done as far as possible through the agency of the people of India. "The aim of England had ever been to raise the inhabitants of India, so that they might be prepared to share this responsibility of Governing India with the British".[25]

* * *

When Charles Metcalfe was ruling in Delhi Britain was in the midst of fighting another world war.[26] When George Everest was surveying the Great Arc and William Sleeman was eradicating the Thugs Britons were settling Australia and continental Canada. When Bartle Frere was cleaning up Bombay Britons were weaning the New Zealand Maoris away from their favourite pastime – eating each other.

---

[25] Bartle Frere's speech in Bombay in 1867 – Sir Bartle Frere and his times by Rekha Ranade p.32

[26] Britain was fighting for her life in a war with revolutionary and Napoleonic France which lasted over twenty years. It has been named the 'second world war'.

The first convict fleet reached Botany Bay in 1788 and they kept coming to New South Wales until 1840 and did not cease in all Australia until 1868. There is some truth in the claim that this continental nation was founded by the disadvantaged, distressed poor criminal class of Britain, but right from the earliest years free settlers as well as convicts went to Australia. From such an unpromising start a vigorous, prosperous and free nation has been planted, nurtured and has matured into one of the most attractive countries on earth. This is no accident and neither is it because the British are a superior people. It is likely because there were enough Godly people in both the mother country and the colonies who were prayerful and working humbly to create a state whose foundation was justice and righteousness.

Canada, named by Jacques Cartier who mistook the Indian word Kannata meaning a collection of huts for the name of the whole country, was brought into the European orbit in 1535 just when England was dissolving the monasteries. For the next 200 years the French and English had an uneasy relationship with the English in the Hudson Bay and New England and the French in the St. Lawrence river basin and creeping down the Ohio river. The rivalry came to a head in the Seven Years war of 1756-63, known by some as the First World War as it was fought all over the world, and in 1763 at the Treaty of Paris all of French North America was ceded to Britain. Canada remained loyal to Britain during the revolutionary war which resulted in the creation of the USA and since the war with America in 1812 has remained at peace with its giant southern neighbour. Canada like America worked its way west during the nineteenth century. The border between the two countries from the Atlantic to the Pacific was completed in 1846 and west of the Great Lakes it is along the 49th parallel of latitude. It is the longest undefended border in the world - something like 5,500 miles. Negotiating the position of this border involving vast territories, was settled calmly and swiftly as both parties were civilised states with a common language, fundamental common interests and common sense[27].

Aotearoa, the Land of the Long White Cloud, was the Maori name for New Zealand. The Maoris migrated from the central Pacific islands to New Zealand in their open long boats about a thousand years ago. This great breed of sea wanderers in their ocean going canoes endured the unexplored vast wastes of the south west pacific, sailing for months on end till they eventually made land fall on one of the most attractive countries on earth. They lived fairly settled lives populating both islands engaging in tribal warfare and cannibalism as they were a warlike people. This way of life went on for several centuries until the coming the 'pakeha' – the white man – about the same time as the convicts arrived in Australia. For several years New Zealand was just a remote dangerous place; a dubious haven for escaped convicts, whalers and seal hunters who chanced cannibal attack. But news of this fertile land got out and bold land hungry and gold hungry spirits started to arrive and men and women with all sorts of skills planted yet another new nation. By the treaty of Waitangi signed in 1840 the Maori chiefs cede their sovereignty to Queen Victoria in return for their

---

27 A History of the American People by Paul Johnson

land guarantees. This imperfect treaty was interpreted differently by the Maoris and the new settlers and land wars erupted in the 1840s and 60s. British settlers brought British ideals and standards and by 1854 a Parliament had been elected bringing responsible self government to the country. There is much that can be said for this small country – the most remote in the world. But this will have to do; it was first country in the world to give women the vote and has provided Britain with wool, fruit, meat and milk products for over a century. The SS Hororata of the New Zealand Shipping Company during the second (fourth!) world war was able to bring enough foodstuff from New Zealand to feed the whole of Britain for a fortnight!

The Gilbert Islands (now known as Kiribati) had few waterside villages before the British Protectorate. This was because there was constant faction warfare, often involving two or three villages at a time, but sometimes splitting whole islands into opposing camps.

For nine generations two factions kept Tarawa, the largest island in the group, in almost continuous fighting. On 27th May 1892 H.M.S Royalist arrived and proclaimed the island a British Protectorate thus ending the unimaginable killing and misery.[28]

* * *

In about 1815 Mountstuart Elphinstone, later to be Governor of Bombay wrote concerning the British Indian

---

[28] *Pattern of Island* by Arthur Grimble

empire, *"The most desirable death for us to die of should be, the improvement of the natives reaching such a pitch as would render it impossible for a foreign nation to retain the government..."* For the nineteenth and the first part of the twentieth centuries there remained a reluctance to grant self government to the subject races, partly out of fear and a natural desire to retain power, but also out of a growing conviction that non white races were inferior and therefore not able to govern themselves. Part of the fruit of Darwin's theory of evolution was the idea of the survival of the fittest and this made discrimination intellectually respectable. So much so that even as late as 1926 it was necessary for a senior member of the Indian Civil Service to write, *"The only way to fit men for responsibility is to place responsibility upon them"*. Responsibility was not being placed upon the non white nations of the empire which meant that after the second world war they took advantage of Britain's exhaustion and bankruptcy to demand independence which was granted often in a hasty haphazard and sometimes bloody way.

The failure of Britain to prepare the non white nations for independence may be illustrated by the observation that in the first decade of the twentieth century Burma, Beluchistan, Zimbabwe, The Sudan and others were better governed than they are a century later.

Britain and the empire paid a price for being seduced by theories which though persuasive and plausible are without substance and at the end of the day destructive.

Racism which is the cardinal sin of early twenty first century grew out of eugenics[29] which was spawned by 'the survival of the fittest' which Charles Darwin gave to the world in his Theory of Evolution in 1859.

---

[29] literally meaning "well born." Eugenics is a genetic and social theory whereby the human race is improved by selective reproduction whereby desirable characteristics are propagated and undesirable traits are eliminated.

Chapter 5

AM I MY BROTHER'S KEEPER?

On 25ᵗʰ March 1807 the Abolition of the Slave Trade bill received the Royal Assent and became law.

Slavery has contaminated human society since the dawn of history. It has polluted almost every nation with its destructive misery. Perhaps the most famous ancient example of slavery is that of the Jews enslaved by the Egyptians about 3500 years ago. Their enslavement is described in a matter of fact way in the Bible in Exodus chapter 1 verse 8,

"Then a new king who did not know Joseph came to power in Egypt. 'Look', he said to his people, 'the Israelites have become too numerous for us. Come we must deal shrewdly with them or they will become even more numerous and, if war breaks out, will join our enemies, fight against us and leave the country'. So they put slave masters over them to

oppress them with forced labour and they built Pithom and Rameses as store cities for pharaoh."

Until two hundred years ago all cultures sanctioned slavery in one form or another. The economy of ancient Greece and Rome was slave based, indeed could not operate without them. They had of course a ready supply in the so called barbarian tribes which were always a source of irritation and which were in easy reach. And warfare was made slightly humane as prisoners were valued as slaves and not simply slaughtered. Slavery was part of the fabric of life and the open slave market existed in backward societies right up to recent decades.

When we talk about slavery today we think about the capture and purchase of human beings from East Africa to be sold into Arabia and the Asia; also from West Africa to be shipped to the Americas. It is this latter trade which has degraded the reputation of so many western nations. The Spanish and Portuguese found the Africans to be well suited to tropical hard labour and began to capture and sell them to the Brazilian and Caribbean planters in the early sixteenth century. The English got into the business about fifty years later. The process was to buy or capture men and women on the West African coast, ship them to the Americas where they were sold in exchange for coffee, sugar, rum etc which found a ready market back in Europe. This went on with little opposition for two hundred years until the second half of the eighteenth century.

The first tentative step in the abolishing of slavery came when in June 1772 Lord Mansfield, Chief Justice of the King's Bench, the highest law court in England, ordered a negro slave, James Somerset, owned by a Mr. Stewart visiting England from Virginia to be set free. This decision was understood to mean that there were to be no slaves in England, although as Lord Mansfield wrote later, "Nothing was more then determined than that there was no right in the master forcibly to take the slave and carry him abroad". The friends of James Somerset, who had been kidnapped by his owner, had sought a writ of Habeas Corpus and he was freed under its ruling.

At around the same time there was a reawakening of Christian conscience through the work of God and the preaching of Whitfield, the Wesley brothers, Jonathan Edwards in New England and others. As a result the Society for the Abolition of the Slave Trade was organised in May 1787 and men like William Wilberforce and Thomas Clarkson worked tirelessly until the Abolition of the Slave Trade bill became law in 1807. These men and women were motivated by high ideals and gave their own money and time to a cause which had much opposition by vested interests entrenched for many centuries. They battled, sometimes at the cost of their own health, and indeed metaphorically moved mountains. Government resources were not part of this initiative; it came from inspired, committed, talented ordinary men and women.

For the British Parliament to abolish the shipping of slaves across the Atlantic ocean, although it took many decades to bring about, was in some ways the easy bit. Many British traders continued the shipment illegally and no European state took up the cause. The abolishing bill in itself would remain little more than a nice idea unless there was the will and the means to implement it. As it turned out the situation in the years following 1807 was remarkably favourable towards abolition of the slave trade. The battle of Trafalgar was fought in 1805 when the Royal Navy won a complete victory over the combined fleets of the two major continental maritime powers, France and Spain. Within ten years of this victory there was little serious work for the Royal Navy to do. It meant that this huge, powerful fighting force could be used for policing the Atlantic coast of Africa and suppressing the slave trade. And this is what happened, although in fits and starts.

The British Admiralty established a permanent West African naval squadron in 1816. This was pitiably small in its early days; far too small given the number of slave ships operating in the countless rivers, inlets and creeks along the West African coast from Gambia south to the Congo river something like 3,500 miles. Even as late as 1827 it is estimated that 10,000 slaves annually were taken from one small area of West Africa alone. From about this time rogue British slavers ceased as slave trading was classified as piracy thus punishable by death.

The British government made great diplomatic efforts to persuade other nations to ban the trade with various degrees of success. The Americans banned the trade at the same time as the British, but their slave traders transferred their ship registrations to other nations which still sanctioned slavery like Spain. France too had followed Britain's lead and abolished the slave trade in 1815, but made no attempt to stop French ships carrying out the trade and even in 1821 many were busy slaving. In spite of intense diplomatic efforts the French refused to allow the Royal Navy to arrest their slave ships even though it was illegal for the French to trade in slaves. Spain too, under pressure from Britain agreed in 1821 that Spanish ships would cease carrying slaves. It was essentially an empty gesture as Spanish ships were re-registered in Cuba and carried on as before. The reluctance of the other Atlantic nations to enforce their anti slave trade laws meant that the burden of suppressing fell on the Royal Navy and the trade went on for many more years than it should.

By the early 1850s the main slaving ports of Whydah and Lagos on the Gulf of Guinea were shut down by the Royal Navy and had turned to the production of equally valuable commodities such as palm oil which meant that the source of slaves dried up and the trans-Atlantic trade withered.

During the years 1808 to 1852 with only a handful of ships, rarely more than 25 at any one time, the Royal Navy African Squadron captured 1200 slave ships and released 140,000 slaves. With the end of the American civil war in 1867 when slavery in the US was abolished the Atlantic slave trade reduced to a trickle.

In 1845 the Sultan of Zanzibar signed a treaty with Britain prohibiting the export of slaves from the East African mainland. This treaty permitted slaves to be brought to Zanzibar to work in the island's clove plantations. However, many more slaves than was needed for local work were brought in and reshipped to the Persian Gulf. This treaty was replaced by one in 1873 when the notorious Zanzibar slave market was closed, demolished and a Christian church built on the site by Bishop Steere of the British Universities Mission to Central Africa. The clandestine trading in slaves went on as before, but this treaty meant that the Royal Navy could take more direct action.

The British East African Squadron waged a continuous fight against the Arab slaving dhows. The squadron was never more than seven ships and patrolled from the Mozambique channel in the south to the coast of Baluchistan in the Arabian sea in the north. It was the same thankless and dangerous story; patrolling the known slave ship routes capturing slavers and releasing their human cargoes.

There is an impressive picture in the National Archives at Kew, taken in 1868, showing the main deck of HMS Daphne crammed with slaves rescued by the Royal Navy from Arab Dhows. It perfectly illustrates the work the navy undertook at that time.

The last known slave dhow in East African waters was captured in 1899, but the traffic went on in Zanzibar until 1907 and in Tanganyika until 1922[30].

If the work of the Royal Navy was unspectacular, routine and unrelenting a dazzling shooting star swept across the upper Nile for a few years in the late 1870's. General Charles Gordon was appointed governor general of the Sudan by the Egyptian ruler Ismail Pasha. Gordon was determined to suppress the slave trade. He arrived in Khartoum in May 1877 and quickly brought together a small band of loyal lieutenants. (He had only accepted the

---

[30] The White Nile by Alan Moorehead p 317

offer of the job in England in February) Immediately he set to work with almost superhuman energy. He established a sound unbribable administration; reorganising taxation and the penal system. He nurtured trade and Khartoum started to flourish and communications with the rest of the region improved. He was determined to stamp out slavery – so engrained in the Sudan as to be thought impossible. In 1878 a slave baron in Darfur raised a formidable army to challenge the new government and in a quick campaign one of Gordon's lieutenants led an expedition which put down the revolt which resulted in the release of ten thousand slaves. At that time the trade in slaves ended and Darfur, Kordofan and the lawless regions enjoyed a short period of peace. Exhausted, Gordon resigned in 1880. In the few years as ruler of the Sudan he had pacified the country with only a handful of helpers. In that time he rode over 8000 miles by camel to the remote reaches of a territory as big as France and Germany combined. He also journeyed to neighbouring countries negotiating peace and trade treaties. Gordon was a man inspired, who held high principles which were not influenced or dependent on political expediency. He was almost other worldly in that when offered a salary of £6000 a year he said that half was more than sufficient. When all is said and done Gordon was God's man. He received guidance, inspiration and comfort from the Bible. He could never have accomplished what he did without the intimate knowledge that he was carrying out God's purpose.

If trading in slaves was an abomination to be abolished then slavery itself should not be tolerated. However, the vested interests in the Caribbean plantations and in

Britain were well entrenched and the idea that slavery had always been around meant that convincing the nation that it was wrong was a formidable task. The Christian conscience of the country was aroused and the action of the anti-slavery Agency Committee which organised mass petitions was committed to unconditional and immediate abolition of slavery. In August 1833 law was passed which called for the gradual abolition of slavery but which required all blacks over the age of six on 1st August 1834 to serve an apprenticeship of up to 6 years. This arrangement proved unsatisfactory and freedom for all Caribbean slaves in British territory was proclaimed in August 1838. Proclamations are easy; implementing good intentions a lot more difficult.

In 1843 the Indian Slavery Act V passed into law and the slave market was banished from British India and the penal code of 1861 made the enslavement of human beings a criminal offence. Sir Bartle Frere who sat on the council of the Governor of India estimated that there were as many as eight or nine million slaves in British India at that time. These were set free by decree.

Nobody likes their property to be taken from them whether it is legal or not. In order to sweeten a bitter pill Parliament voted twenty million pounds to compensate the West Indian planters. No such scheme was provided for the slave owners in India. Many slaves in India exchanged slavery for debt bondage. This meant that low caste Indians who previously would have been regarded as slaves continued working for their erstwhile owners in exchange for sometimes less than their subsistence. It was step in the right direction, but it could mean that debt passed down the generations effectively tying workers and their children to their employer.

Vested interests in the form of greed, selfishness and particularly an unwillingness to acknowledge that all persons are made in the image of God and therefore precious prevailed in all nations, including Britain. These interests applied immense pressure to allow slavery to continue. And it has.

Slavery has now gone underground - it has even changed its name to 'people trafficking'.

Organised crime gangs are able to bring vulnerable mainly young women into all western nations, including Britain, with vague false promises of a 'better life' and then openly sell them in deals made in airport environs cafes. This is known about and sometimes publicised with understandable horror and much hand wringing. Little is done except a government or European statement deploring the situation. A sense of helpless impotence prevails resulting in the public representatives of those in power frantically attempting to be seen to be doing something. This results in the all too common round of conferences, press releases, media interviews all deploring the situation from a moral high ground coupled with a demand for money from the state.

* * *

Britain's contribution to ridding open slavery from the world has been played down. Britain, inspired by the evangelistic Christian conscience played, not just a leading role, but fought the trade alone for several decades often with the covert hostility of many hypocritical nations which nominally banned slavery themselves.

Britain prevailed in not just banning the slave trade and decreeing that the enslavement of human beings be a criminal offence in the territories under her control. She also eventually persuaded and cajoled all other nations to do the same. It was a great act requiring clarity of vision, a sense of moral purpose, a willingness to pay whatever price necessary and a quality of long suffering perseverance. It also required the determination to do what was right even when the rest of the world was indifferent or hostile. It required most of all the commitment of praying people who believed that God was as fed up as they were with His fallen creation and who was willing to get involved with a solution only when His people cared enough to ask Him for help.

Why is Britain's role played down? Maybe it is not possible to emulate the nineteenth century spirit today because the only tool seemingly available is money. In the public sphere patience is in short supply as instant results are required by those directing funds. The immensity of the problem is also overwhelming, as humanly speaking trafficking is too deeply rooted for any agency to solve. Thus frustrated impotence coupled with a challenged conscience brings little more than a poisonous mix of hysteria, self deception and depression. This comes about because few people are willing to emulate Wilberforce, Clarkson etc and bring God into the question and without them the slave market could well exist in all nations.

Chapter 6

Screws and Loos

Why bother with machines when you have slaves or a caste system or serfs or a despised servant class to do the repetitive, monotonous, exhausting and dirty work. That has been the attitude of humanity for countless centuries. Indeed there seems to be a bias in human nature towards this state. When as early as the first century the Greek engineer Heron invented a viable steam engine[31] it was regarded as a toy; it was never developed and put to work. And as Van Loon's Law[32] states, *"The amount of mechanical development will always be in inverse ratio to the number of*

---

[31] He called his device "aeolipile," which means "wind ball" in Greek. The steam was supplied by a sealed cauldron filled with water and placed over a fire. Two tubes came up from the pot, letting the steam flow into a spherical ball of metal. The metallic sphere had two curved outlet tubes, which directed the steam into two jets so that the metal sphere rotated. The Greeks never used this remarkable device for anything but a toy.

[32] See 'The story of mankind' by Hendrik Van Loon

slaves that happen to be at a country's disposal". The Greeks had an adequate supply of slaves.

By the seventeenth century things began to change. The Reformation brought the availability of the Bible and an eagerness to read. With this came the understanding that anyone could think for himself and this made a big impression in protestant Europe, especially in England. The idea that all mankind were created in the image of God and therefore of equal value was disturbing for the privileged classes, but all levels of society were exposed to the liberating Christian gospel and these ideas took root.

Applied science was gaining influence all over Europe and by the middle of the seventeenth century just after the restoration of the English monarchy following the significant political upheavals of the Commonwealth period, the Royal Society was founded. This stimulated enquiry in all sorts of scientific fields and the results were made widely available.

In the late 1600s an ironmonger from Dartmouth in Devon named Thomas Newcomen struggled for many years to try to overcome the problem of pumping water from deep mines which were being sunk all over Britain. The cost of using horse and man power was prohibitive and of course slaves were not available. Newcomen was inspired by the idea of using steam to operate a pump and was determined to apply the ideas of the French Huguenot Denis Papin (who came to live in England and was admitted to the Royal Society). He worked with his neighbour John Calley who was a master plumber and together they built a simple model of Papin's idea operating a rocking beam; one end attached to the piston in a cylinder and the other working a pump. The power was achieved by allowing steam to fill the cylinder and push the piston out, then condensing the steam and creating a vacuum which caused atmospheric pressure to push the piston back into the cylinder. The condensing process was very slow and inefficient until by "a special act of providence" water accidentally enter the steam cylinder causing a rapid condensing of the steam and the piston came down with such force that it broke from its chain and crushed not only the bottom of the cylinder but the top of the boiler below. "Thus did the Almighty present mankind with one of the most wonderful inventions which has ever been brought into the light of day."[33] Using this rapid condensing effect Newcomen built and installed the first effective steam rocking beam engine used for pumping water from deep mines at Dudley Castle in Staffordshire in 1712. It was an instant success and about a further 100 were built over the next 20 years in all parts of the country.

A working version of the Newcomen engine (probably built in the later eighteenth century) was acquired in 1963 and erected in the Newcomen Museum in Dartmouth and is known as the Newcomen Memorial Engine. It is worth a visit. A plaque states:

"The unprecedented innovation of the steam-atmospheric engine (c 1712) by Thomas Newcomen (1663-1729) of Dartmouth, England and his assistant John Calley, stands at

---

[33] Martin Triewald, who worked with Newcomen in building engines.

the beginning of the development of practical thermal prime movers in the world.

It was indeed one of the strategic innovations in world history and the single greatest act of synthesis in the ensuing history of the steam engine.

This engine is representative of the Newcomen line of engines."

"In 1710 the very inventive Mr. Newcomen was called to the ministry and he became the Baptist Minister for Dartmouth. He was active in the church up to his death in 1729".[34]

During the remainder of the eighteenth century the atmospheric engine was used in many parts of the world. Although improved by James Watt and others it remained large, cumbersome and slow. It was also inefficient. Now at the end of the century the Cornishman Richard Trevithick appeared on the scene. He worked using high pressure steam which resulted in much smaller, more efficient and faster engines. In 1802 he built a road locomotive which he drove from Redruth in Cornwall to Plymouth, a distance of about 60 miles. Two years later Trevithick built the first steam locomotive to run on rails. This engine hauled 10 tons of iron, 70 passengers and five wagons nine miles from the Penydarren mine in South Wales to the Merthyr-Cardiff canal at a speed of five miles an hour. The heavy engine and its wagons put too much strain on the cast iron rails which frequently broke thus making these early locomotives commercially unviable.

---

[34]   A plaque in the Newcomen museum in Dartmouth.

There followed many experiments with steam powered locomotion, most noteworthy that by William Hadley with his Puffing Billy (now in the Science Museum in London) which also proved too heavy for the rails of the time.

It was not until a quarter century later that technology caught up with the inventors. During these years the need for cheap transportation of coal from the Durham pits to the coastal ports was becoming more and more urgent. The prosperous Quaker merchant Edward Pease proposed a horse drawn railway and with a group of business friends setup the Stockton to Darlington Railway Company and they applied for an Act of Parliament to acquire land and implement the scheme. Pease was persuaded by George Stephenson that the railway should be powered by steam rather than horses and Robert Stephenson and Company of Newcastle upon Tyne became the worlds first locomotive builder. By 1825 the line was complete and the engine named 'Locomotion' pulled 12 wagons of freight and 20 wagons of passengers and the nine mile journey took 2 hours. From this time the railway ran every day except Sundays for several years.

And in 1829 George and Robert Stephenson's famous 'Rocket' lived up to its name when it won the Rainhill trials reaching a speed of 24 mph over a 20 lap track and demonstrated that reliable, reasonably efficient, fairly lightweight mechanical locomotion was viable. Since that time transportation has never looked back.

Not only transport; mechanical power was applied to the repetitive monotonous processes like spinning and weaving such that in a very short time large power driven mills were springing up all over the country which provided high quality relatively cheap goods to ordinary people; goods which beforehand were reserved for the wealthy.

Why was it that these inventions should be made in Britain? The engineers, craftsmen and scientists in France, Germany, Italy, Spain, China and other countries were equally talented if not more so. There are several answers.

Firstly and probably most important, was the cultural environment which allowed people with initiative to cultivate their ideas and communicate them to those with a like mind. In England there was an intellectual openness which allowed ideas to flourish. This was in contrast to the continental powers where the state had its heavy hand over too much of individual activity. There is a tendency in all human society for those in power to assume that all wisdom belongs to them and any ideas and thinking which does not meet with their approval are disdained and discarded. It was the liberating intellectual and spiritual climate engendered by the Christian Gospel which made it possible for this favourable fertile environment to come into being, not because of English genius, but because enough people in these islands were committed to truth in an absolute sense and were willing to think new thoughts and explore new ideas and processes.

Secondly the rule of law ensured that state officials were prohibited from meddling in the affairs of ordinary people and this coupled with a surprisingly low level of state corruption allowed some citizens to accumulate considerable wealth. These surplus funds sought opportunities for investment and the new inventions needed the money. Economic and political liberty came first; industrialisation and general wealth followed.

Money and ideas on their own are not enough. It requires a special sort of perseverance, commitment and longsuffering to face down the setbacks, disappointments, loneliness and failed trials and experiments to fight through and overcome – to bring an abstract idea to reality. These virtues are not unique to Christians, all humanity has the potential to rise to great heights. What is unique to a Christian culture is the environment of encouragement surrounding an innovator in which ideas are nurtured. An inventor in Britain up to the middle of the twentieth century was willed to succeed and no artificial impediments were put in his way. Negative advice was disdained and there was a will to succeed which was not always linked to the desire for financial gain. The Christian virtues of courage, hope and humility together with the faith that God's universe was rational and good and full of clues helped clear the dense undergrowth of corrupt obscurantism.

*   *   *

Born near Manchester two years before Nelson fought Trafalgar, Joseph Whitworth, the son of a Congregational minister, worked as a mechanic from an early age. He was aware of the indifferent quality of manufactured goods at the time and resolutely set out to raise standards. Despite derision from many manufacturers, he was determined to improve on the shoddy technology of the day. 'You tell me it can't be done' he told them, but I give you these 3 words, 'Let us try', which became his motto[35]. Whitworth learnt his trade from Henry Maudsley a London engineer who had built a lathe which could cut screws of any diameter and pitch and made precision screw manufacture possible. While with Maudsley in London Whitworth was working alongside other young men destined for fame, such as James Nasmyth (1808-1890), inventor of the steam hammer, and Richard Roberts (1789-1864), inventor of a self-acting spinning mule.

It was not until 1841 after noting that there was no standard for screws (each manufacturer had his own design) that Whitworth proposed and specified a standard pitch for a given diameter, depth, shape and an angle of 55 degrees. This was accepted by the Institution of Civil Engineers and having been adopted by the railways quickly became a national standard. It spread throughout the world and was established as the British Standard Whitworth (BSW). This was his first big breakthrough and this led to the micrometer which could accurately and repeatedly measure down to one thousandth part of an inch.

Up to the 1830s a skilled mechanic could be expected to work to an accuracy of 1/16 inch. But within a few years, thanks to Joseph Whitworth, an accuracy of 1/10,000 of an inch was practical. Modern engineering was born.

In the summer of 1858 there was the Great London Stink when the river Thames was so full of raw sewage

---

[35] Derbyshire UK – Derbyshire on the Internet

that people could not bear to stay in the city. Parliament was sitting through much of this time, though MPs planned to evacuate to Hampton Court. The unbearable stench concentrated the minds of the Members and they immediately appointed a committee to recommend a solution to the problem which had been getting worse for several decades.

Edwin Chadwick, a sanitary engineer supported the claims of the ancient Jewish laws of Moses by stating that "it forbade even an open camp be defiled with human ordure, and expressly ordained that it should be deposited at a distance and immediately covered with soil". He had been promoting the benefits of clean water and the quick removal of sewage for decades. The Great Stink caused Parliament to release funds to provide a comprehensive sewage system for London. The engineer Joseph Bazalgette took charge of the project of building an 83 mile main sewer to carry the effluent down stream from the city to Barking. He also supervised the building of 1100 miles of street sewers. This revolutionized and cleaned up the streets and the river Thames. Peoples homes on the other hand, still stank and did not improve until Thomas Crapper invented the syphonic flush lavatory as we know it and which is used throughout the world. The water closet, or 'WC' as it became known, had been in use for some years, but these early designs needed an excessive quantity of water to flush away the solid waste, some even used a constant flow of water. Even Britain with its generous rainfall did not have sufficient water to serve these lavatories so they never became common and were only available in a few homes. Thomas Crapper developed and enhanced the floating ball valve which allowed water to flow into a cistern and when it was full the ball would close the valve shutting off the water supply. However, his most significant development was the

"Crapper's valveless waste preventer.
One moveable part only.
Certain flush with only one pull.
Will flush when only two thirds full"[36]

A small chamber, open at the bottom to allow water to enter and closed at the top end of the down pipe to the lavatory basin, contained a plate attached to a lever. When the lever is pressed the plate is raised and water is lifted over the top of the down pipe. This produces a siphon action which draws the remaining water from the cistern and rapidly flushes the lavatory pan. Only the precise amount of water in the cistern is used and no more flushes can be made until the cistern fills again. This process together with the invention of the 'U' bend brought hygiene into homes and the killer diseases like typhoid and cholera were banished from British cities. The principles of good sanitation quickly spread to all parts of the world.

Michael Faraday from a humble family – the son of a blacksmith – with only elementary formal education became one the most famous scientists ever. At 13 years old he left school and found work as an apprentice to a bookbinder whose books he enthusiastically read. Faraday's

---

[36] Flushed with Pride by Wallace Reyburn – page 13

humble beginnings make a life in science improbable but maybe the family's Christian commitment made all the difference. They were members of the Sandemanians, a small Christian group who believed that the truth of the Bible was to be recovered by as literal a reading as possible and made Christ central to the conduct of their lives. His belief required that he express his faith in the smallest details of everyday life as well as the greatest.[37]

By 1820s Faraday was established at the Royal Institution where he was appointed superintendent of laboratories and where he worked for the next forty years. Working with Humphry Davy he discovered the connection between electricity and magnetism. They discovered that an electric current has magnetic properties by Faraday making a current carrying wire circulate around a fixed magnet. This principle was developed into the electric motor. He also showed the opposite effect where a magnet moving through a coil of wire will generate a voltage. This led to the dynamo or electric generator and the

---

[37]   As a Sandemanian Faraday would not accept that the book of nature is written in a language so removed from experience as the language of mathematics. Theories could be admired and used but to him they were more tinged with humanity than with the divine. Sandemanian suspicion of theology and mathematical abstraction suggested that those come between observers and the book of nature. This is why Faraday insisted on separating the discussion of religious from scientific matters. In a lecture given in 1854 in the presence of Prince Albert, he argued that their humanity makes all people-including scientists-'active promoters of error.' How, then, is scientific knowledge possible? The Sandemanian element in his Christianity promised that, like the Bible, the book of nature would be open to anyone who sought to read it without prejudice.   From http://www.bath.ac.uk/~hssdcg/Michael_Faraday.html

transformer. Faraday developed field theory that was in conflict with the mathematical theories of the age which were being promoted by his more famous contemporaries. His non conforming religion was mirrored in his non conforming physics and his commitment to the validity of observation even when it conflicted with predicting theory allowed him to 'think outside the box' and bring into being the concepts of electromagnetic induction and radiation which were established by him and his successors during the nineteenth century. Although his Sandemanian Christianity made Faraday distrust mathematical interpretations of nature, it encouraged him to pursue the path of observation and experiment and to base his theories on qualitative imagery. In following that path Faraday discovered a unity of activity and purpose that few people achieve in any walk of life. [38]

While Whitworth was developing his micrometer and Faraday wrestling with force fields, Charles Babbage was struggling to construct his Difference Engine and designing the Analytical Engine. The purpose of the Difference Engine was to calculate mathematical tables used for navigation. It was never completed for personal and financial reasons. The Analytical Engine was the mechanical ancestor of the modern computer and his original design, never constructed in Babbage's lifetime, was built in 1991 to commemorate the 200th anniversary of his birth.

---

[38] Much of this section on Faraday is from David Gooding of University of Bath

It is noteworthy that Babbage received some of his education at the Grammar School in Totnes which is at the tidal head of the river Dart. Thus the Dart valley has nurtured two earth shaking inventions which have blessed and revolutionised the whole world: Newcomen's steam engine and Babbage's computer.

Chapter 7

'DON'T MENTION THE WAR'

Next to a battle lost, the greatest misery is a battle won.
The Duke of Wellington

It is difficult for Christians to justify war - it is probably impossible to justify. However, in a world where imperfection is the norm, warfare is a fact of life. And greed, selfishness, pride and fear motivate much of the policy of all nations making it necessary for everyone to pass judgement on their own and other countries. This requires qualities of character necessary to discern good from evil; wisdom to weigh facts and pass correct judgement; courage to make hard and painful decisions - such as going to war: perseverance to see a conflict through dark times to the right conclusion. Historically Britain has displayed these qualities to a remarkable degree.

In whatever form warfare takes it is always destructive, fearful and brutal - bringing death and immeasurable misery to countless people. In spite of being most vile it is endemic in all humanity and makes a lie that the human race is moving ever onwards and upwards to a more advanced state.

Warfare like blood sacrifices is universal and found in all tribes, cultures and nations from the beginning of history. The people of the British Isles being no exception have been amongst the most active in fighting and killing. From the earliest times when Queen Boadica led the Iceni tribes of Southern Britain against the Roman invaders through the centuries when the aggressive tribes of Angles, Saxons, Vikings, Danes and Normans fought for these islands there has been a warlike spirit in Britain. Since the Norman conquest this aggressive spirit has been mostly directed towards the outside world. In the hundred years war, ending in the mid 1400s, it was almost an annual event for adventurous young men to go the France for a few months after the harvest to fight, ravish and pillage.

In the 200 years since 1800 Britain has fought against or in the territory of some 36 countries throughout the world.

> Portugal
> Spain
> France
> Italy
> Belgium
> Holland
> Denmark
> Norway
> Germany
> Russia

Austria
Greece
Turkey
Syria
Palestine
Egypt
Sudan
Ethiopia
Libya
Tunisia
Algeria
Morocco
South Africa
Madagascar
Yemen
Iraq
Persia
Afghanistan
India
Burma
China
Malaya
Korea
Japan
Argentina
USA

The influence of the Christian gospel occasionally softened the edge of European aggression until the reformation when Roman Catholics and Protestants came into conflict. The deeply held convictions of opposing belief systems led to intense bitterness and vicious killing and in 1588 Spain launched her armada determined to bring protestant England back into the catholic fold. A combination of good English tactics, poor Spanish leadership and finally a strong south westerly storm dispersed the Spanish fleet which limped home having lost more than half its ships. The English government struck a medal with the inscription *"God blew and they were scattered"* and from that time English maritime power grew to eventually dominate the oceans of the world.

Britain has been involved in countless conflicts large and small since the armada, some within these islands, many in Europe and something like 50 in all parts of the world in Queen Victoria's reign alone, but those which have had the biggest impact on the country have been the four global wars between Britain and the maritime powers of France, Spain and latterly Germany and Japan. The first of these four world wars was the 7 years war, fought in the mid 1700s, when Britain broke the power of France in eastern North America and in India. The next was fought around the opening years of the nineteenth century against revolutionary and Napoleonic France which sought to impose a tyrannical ideology on all of Europe. The twentieth century saw the emergence of Germany followed by Japan as major industrial powers whose totalitarian governments sought to impose their proud corrupt ideologies on their neighbours.

The motive for these global wars was complex and mixed. Some were territorial, some ideological, all from baser motives such as pride, envy, greed and fear, but probably a mixture of all these plus other reasons which are too painful to acknowledge or beyond human understanding played their part.

Britain emerged from all these conflicts victorious. This can be regarded as a miracle as Britain was matched against formidable foes commanding huge resources. All saw Britain as a major obstacle to their world dominating ambitions who had to be defeated. Britain's enemies all built strong naval forces but the work of the Royal Navy and latterly the Royal Air Force in preventing an invasion is an epic and inspiring story.

At least two of these conflicts were essentially ideological in that Britain was fighting to prevent a determined foe from dominating continental Europe and imposing totalitarian dictatorship on all nations. The first was against revolutionary and Napoleonic France who had succeeded in subduing all the continental nations but whose power was broken by Britain's command of the sea. Britain came out of this conflict victorious and the most powerful nation on earth. The war lasted over 20 years and Britain fought often alone against a determined, devious and deceitful foe, yet was able to build coalitions on seven separate occasions from various disaffected conquered continental countries. These coalitions came about because Britain was wealthy enough to finance huge continental armies which three times out of four were destroyed by Napoleon. 22 years of almost continuous war leaving between 5 and 6 million dead had reduced continental Europe to exhaustion and poverty. Britain persevered and finally overcame France and came out of the war even more wealthy and dominated the world stage for the next 100 years.

Britain's army was small by continental standards, but played a major part by holding down something like 300,000 of Napoleon's best troops in Spain and Portugal. The Royal navy was Britain's strongest arm which made it impossible for France to invade. French and Spanish ships were of high quality, but they lacked seamanship and leadership. The Royal Navy employed men of character exemplified by Nelson's Band of Brothers and these led and inspired reluctant pressed men to acts of selflessness and sacrifice. The persevering 'British Bulldog' came from this time. This period also saw the rapid advancement of the industrial revolution which made Britain the workshop of the world.

The other great ideological war was the Second World War and of all the many participating nations only Britain and her daughter nations were in it from start to finish. Nazi Germany was determined to not only change the political map of Europe and maybe the world, but to impose a way of life on all its subject people which would have meant returning to the dark ages of slavery and racial obliteration.

Even in the early twenty first century when we say 'the war' we mean the Second World War, even though since 1945 Britain has fought several wars either alone or in coalition and almost a ceaseless policing role all over the world. The Second World War was the war which affected the whole world.

Britain's enemy Germany had on balance better war equipment. At sea the British excelled in numbers of ships, but the Germans had the edge in quality. Their pocket battleships outclassed our equivalent. The Royal

Air Force had better quality aircraft; eg the Spitfire and Lancaster, but the Germans had greater numbers. The German army was superbly equipped. Right up to the end of the war the tanks of the western allies were no match for the German Tiger and Panther. The German machine gun the MG42 was highly reliable with a phenomenal firing rate of 1200 rounds per minute and was probably the best general purpose machine gun ever made.

How is it that a small island nation managed to challenge aggressive rivals who often with much forethought had prepared, equipped and trained large forces long before hostilities broke out; some like revolutionary France and Nazi Germany who were driven by corrupt ideologies motivating whole nations to extreme passions?

Being an island helped, but that did not help Madagascar, Cyprus or Japan. The British were not better warriors than other nations as in the opening stages of major wars she was unprepared and often poorly led and equipped and suffered serious setbacks. Definitely not a superior race as the British are very much a mongrel people.

So could there be another aspect which contributes to this unique story? Maybe the spiritual dimension has an important impact. The trouble is, the mention of anything spiritual in a personal or national life creates the same kind of intense horrific embarrassment as is associated with the mention of sex in a prudish emotionally suppressed Victorian household. The emotionally crippled atheistic intellectual club simply can't cope and as they dominate British thinking the nation is unable to look at itself and its history in a balanced and realistic way with much pride as well some shame.

The history of British warfare is understandably dominated by the major world wars which took such an immense toll of lives. However, in 1945 the world entered the nuclear age where just one bomb could, and did, destroy a whole major city and this means the nature of warfare will never be the same. Gone forever are massed armies and large naval fleets. Never again will an aggressive continental power mobilise tens of thousands of troops on the frontier of a smaller neighbour such as Belgium or Poland. Of course, this does not mean that warfare itself is a thing of the past, it just means that the form of warfare has changed. Men will always disagree with each other and these disagreements will often degenerate into violence as one group seeks to impose its views on another.

The consignment of conventional warfare to the dustbin of history means that much can be learnt from how the British waged small wars in the past in order to pacify lawless regions. This experience is in contrast with the heavy handed approach adopted by the Americans and British in Iraq and Afghanistan in the early twenty first century. The example of Herbert Edwardes in Bannu is worthy of a closer study.

* * *

Herbert Edwardes was one of about 30 of the dedicated band of young men recruited by Henry Lawrence to administer the Punjab under a Council of Regency after the first Sikh war in 1847. These passionate young men had great responsibilities placed on them and given great freedom to carry them out. And in the words of Philip Mason in his history 'The men who ruled India' *they scoured the country, advising, exhorting and from time to time firmly, and without any authority, taking things into their own hands. 'The protection of the people against the oppression of the Sikh Collectors will be your first duty' wrote Lawrence to one of them.*

The doings of Herbert Edwardes in Bannu are the best example of what happened in those days. The Afghans had ceded Bannu to the Sikhs but neither had ever administered this high desolate valley, where every man went armed and no one had ever willingly paid a tax. Every three years the Sikhs sent an army to punish the Bannuchis for their failure to pay tribute; they lived on the valley, burnt the crops they did not eat, carried off the cattle and brought back not a third of one year's revenue. The time came to send out another of these punitive expeditions. Sir Henry Lawrence agreed, but on condition that a British political officer went too and tried to make a peaceful settlement. The Sikhs smiled and agreed; Herbert Edwardes set out, the only Englishman with an army of Sikhs – recently defeated. He was not even in command. But he began by enforcing an order that the army must pay for everything.

This transformed the situation. The Bannuchis were astonished by an army that did not plunder; they came and talked. They sold provisions to the army. Night after night they came to Edwardes tent and sat talking to him about the terms on which they might agree to pay revenue peacefully. In the end he went away without his agreement, but he

*had promised to come back for a longer stay and next year
when he came for three months he achieved miracles. They
dismantled their forts; they agreed to pay a reduced land
revenue and he began a field by field survey which would
lead to an accurate assessment. Finally he decided that they
needed a legal code and wrote it one night. He turned it into
Persian next day and made a beginning of administering his
code single handed. The Political Adviser became judge as
well as financier, tax gatherer, commander in chief, engineer
and legislator – Moses as well as Napoleon.*

Character is paramount. Clear, confident, experienced and
firm leadership which can mobilise serious and effective
armed force yet keep it on a tight leash is fundamentally
important to any protagonist hoping to prevail in any
conflict. If at the same time this leadership can put in the
front line a small number of the right sort of men, then
these gifted men who have a clear objective and aim can
be given the responsibility to bring a fair and peaceful
settlement. This happened in Bannu and other places.
It could happen in the twenty first century, but is more
difficult for a number of reasons. Firstly, with instant
communications any campaign is run by the 'experts' at
the head office base and these people generally do not
trust their subordinates and suffer from lack of nerve.
Also the men on the ground are not given a free hand
and sense the mistrust of their superiors. The principle
driving the Lawrence brothers and their contemporaries
was that they would always back their men on the ground.
(If mistakes were made they were sorted out afterwards)
Herbert Edwardes knew he had their backing. Clarity
and character are in short supply these days and thus
confidence and a sense of rightness is missing, so dealing

with lawless peoples is such that our opponents think their way of life – often steeped in poverty and violence- is of equal value to our own.

Conflict will always be with us and much can be learned from British experience.

Chapter 8

WORD GAMES

Word ….

Thousands of homes throughout Britain are host to people from most of the nations on earth; Germany, Spain, Arabia, Korea, Ukraine, Japan, Sweden, Switzerland, Italy, Libya – and this is a list of just some countries whose people come to an obscure small West of England town. And they come to learn the English language.

English, as we know it, did not exist until about the year1400 when Middle English evolved into Modern English. It does not have the ancient pedigree of languages such Hebrew, Greek and Latin.

An Australian, a Briton, a New Zealander, a North American, a Southern African and people from many other countries can go almost anywhere in the world and there will always be someone who will speak to him in English- his native tongue: not grudgingly, but eagerly, because people value the English language and welcome the opportunity to speak it.

More people speak Chinese as their mother tongue than any other. English comes second. However, more people speak, understand and communicate in English that any other by far. Many reasons are given for this; it is the mother tongue of the current super power, the USA. It is the language of the scientific world, the internet and international communications. The rise of industrialisation, commencing in the late seventeenth century largely in Britain, demanded many new words to describe new processes and activities such as engineer, kiosk, business, career, induction, charge, consumer, blog, etc.

English has a larger vocabulary than any other language in that it has a seemingly insatiable appetite for new words, importing them from Norse, Norman French and then Italy, Germany, India, Spain etc. as well as making them up. The Oxford English Dictionary has about a half a million words.

According to the website of the English Language Guide[39] English is listed as the official or co-official language of over 45 countries and is spoken extensively in other countries where it has no official status. English plays a major part in the cultural, political or economic life of the countries shown in the table below. The majority English speaking populations are shown in bold.

---

[39]   See www.englishlanguageguide.com/english/facts/history/

Antigua
Australia
Bahamas
Barbados
Belize
Bermuda
Botswana
Brunei (with Malay)
Cameroon (with French)
Canada (with French)
Dominica
Fiji
Gambia
Ghana
Grenada
Guyana
India (with several Indian languages)
Ireland (with Irish Gaelic)
Jamaica
Kenya (with Swahili)
Kiribati
Lesotho (with Sotho)
Liberia
Malawi (with Chewa)
Malta (with Maltese)
Mauritius
Namibia (with Afrikaans)
Nauru (with Nauruan)

New Zealand
Nigeria
Pakistan (with Urdu)
Papua New Guinea
Philippines (with Tagalog)
Puerto Rico (with Spanish)
St Christopher and Nevis
St Lucia
St Vincent
Senegal (with French)
Seychelles (with French)
Sierra Leone
Singapore (with Malay, Mandarin and Tamil)
South Africa (with Afrikaans, Xhosa and Zulu)
Surinam (with Dutch)
Swaziland (with Swazi)
Tanzania (with Swahili)
Tonga (with Tongan)
Trinidad and Tobago
Tuvalu
Uganda
United Kingdom and its dependecies
United States of America and its dependencies
Vanatu (with French)
Western Samoa (with Samoan)
Zambia
Zimbabwe

The British nations burst into flower with the reformation and with the translation of the Bible into English in 1611 never looked back.

The Bible throughout pursues a remarkable and unusual theme. Names and words are highly regarded; they are important. In the opening verses of the Bible, *God said, "Let there be light," and there was light*[40]. Christians believe God spoke the universe into being. Words are therefore very powerful. Hence, "The pen is mightier than the sword".

Names are also significant. God changed Abram's name to Abraham[41]. The understanding that words and names are important has challenged English scholars for centuries and consequently the definition of many words has been well thought through with precision.

Since the reformation some of the best legal and theological brains have toiled to extract the accurate meaning of many words, and countless books have been written to bring light and reason to bear on the definition of much of the English language. An example is words such as *Justice* and *Righteousness*. The earliest meaning comes from Hebrew, Greek and Latin. The Jews had only one word '*tsedaqah*' for these two and classical Greek also has one '*diakiosis*' and the Romans '*iusticia*'. The English meanings have been forged in the furnace of disputation from ancient texts and everyday experience and need. This took place mainly in the time since the reformation where thinking people sought to bring precision and clarity. This exactness has had a significant

---

[40] The Bible - Genesis Chap 1 Verse 3

[41] The Bible - Genesis Chap 17 Verse 5

impact on the English language generally and biblical understanding and English law particularly and helped justify the position the English language has in the world today.

* * *

In recent decades there has grown up a tendency for political groups to hi-jack and manipulate words to their own ends. An example of this is *compassion* which describes an individual who can show fellow feeling or pity. It is a private virtue. In the 1970s it was manipulated by interest groups and forced to work as the 'compassionate society'. This meant that the phrase came to refer to a public virtue and the meaning became distorted and served only what its inventors wanted it to mean. In reality it meant nothing, as for example, an individual police officer may be compassionate, but the department of state the Home Office can not. Compassion is not a corporate virtue.

Another example is *progressive*. We have the 'progressive society' the use of which identifies its exponents as worthy people which means everyone is obliged to pay lip service to something which is made to mean whatever the speaker or hearer wishes. One is never told what the destination of the progress is!

Yet another example is *justice*. There is 'Global justice', 'Social justice' and lots of other sorts of justice peculiar to interest groups who define justice as anything which supports and enhances their own position. The word justice being hyphenated has been degraded, and hijacked. It has become an emotive term for promoting a special interest.

These phrases are overused and abused, fall out of fashion and are then discarded. Thus sturdy worthwhile words are weakened and important concepts and ideas are lost. This careless use of words comes from a careless hedonistic worldview and damages any language.

Words deserve better as does all manipulated language.

.... games

For when the one Great Sorcerer comes to write against your name
He writes not how you won or lost but how you played the game.

The sport section of a British national paper on a usual Monday devotes over 30 pages to sport. Typically over a dozen different sports are reported on, most in great detail.

Of these four are British sports exported to the world. They are cricket, golf, rugby league and union and football. Most of the remainder have had their rule books drawn in Britain.

They are all competitive games where individuals or teams compete against each other and the outcome is a winner and loser – a concept alien to cultures where revenge is sought for the slightest shame.

In England football was common in the middle ages when the men from one village attempted to kick a ball from one end to the other of a rival village which naturally was determined to stop them. There were no rules; you could not only kick the ball, but carry it; there were no limit to the number, age or sex of people on either side; and there was no such thing as a foul. The matches were more like a riot than a game and bruises, broken bones and bloody heads were more common than not. Medieval football was so violent that in the early 1300,s the Lord Mayor of London banned it. It popularity and its brutality is reflected in the fact that in the late middle ages there were more than 30 national and local laws banning the game.

Francis Willoughby FRS the distinguished seventeenth century polymath was the first known person to define and lay down basic rules for a more civilised version of football. He described a pitch with 'gates' each end and the rival teams attempted and fought to score the first goal by getting the ball through the opponents 'gate'. There was no mention of a referee! In the nineteenth century the English public schools, particularly Eton and Rugby decided that active sports was a valuable part of education, developing the muscles, minds and character of boys, so the rules of football were written down in detail to encourage a fair competitive game. Eventually in 1863 the Football Association was established and this body adopted the Cambridge University rules which were accepted nationwide and which banned handling the ball.

The Football Association rules are basic to all soccer games throughout the world and football has been called yet another great British export.

As early as the 1820s football as played at Rugby school allowed the handling of the ball but not running with it. William Webb-Ellis is credited with picking up the ball and running with it to his opponent's goal and this became an accepted part of the game and was formally incorporated into the rules at Rugby in 1845. It was initially a schools game and the rules of Rugby school dominated mainly because of the reputation of that school. Although not as ubiquitous as soccer, Rugby is a serious international game especially in the southern hemisphere commonwealth countries and is growing in popularity not only among European countries but also in the Far East and the Pacific. Rugby has also influenced American football and Australian rules football.

Rugby League split from Rugby Union in the late nineteenth century when many of the northern clubs who paid their players for loss of earnings were accused of 'professionalism' by the rigidly amateur clubs mainly in southern England. Ironically 100 years after the split Rugby Union allowed professional players. Perhaps the rift can be healed!

Another game England has given to the world is cricket. Men of all classes in eighteenth century England played cricket, although the origins of the game are lost in the early history. Although in the early years the rules were not established and widely recognized, formal competitive games were being played. Cricket was subject to rules laid down by the Marylebone Cricket

Club – the MCC – in the 1830s and became somewhat of a socially stratified game. The MCC and the county clubs becoming professional and the popular game being played on countless amateur grounds all over England and Wales. Cricket is an unusual game as matches can last as long as 5 days, with each side having two "innings", or turns to bat. In recent years shorter games have also been introduced with 20 or 40 'overs'.

Cricket has been exported to the Commonwealth countries and an International Cricket Council – the ICC – administers the game; it is particularly popular in India, Pakistan, the West Indies Australia etc.

Cricket has a mystique, even an obscurity, as the outcome of a game is determined by many factors – some outside the game such as the weather! The following humorous description of the game illustrates how it can be confusing if you are not familiar with the rules.

The Rules of Cricket as explained to a foreign visitor

You have two sides, one out in the field and one in.

Each man that's in the side that's in, goes out, and when he's out, he comes in and the next man goes in until he's out.

When they are all out the side that's out comes in and the side that's been in goes out and tries to get those coming in out.

Sometimes you get men still in and not out.

When both sides have been in and out including the not-outs, that's the end of the game.

Howzat?

All these sports have a universal appeal – all humanity has taken them for their own.

Chapter 9
MISSIONARIES

IN MEMORY OF
JOHN COLERIDGE PATTESON DD
MISSIONARY BISHOP
BORN IN LONDON APRIL 1 1827
KILLED AT NUKAPU NEAR THE ISLAND
OF SANTA CRUZ SEPTEMBER 20 1871
TOGETHER WITH TWO FELLOW WORKERS
FOR OUR LORD THE REV JOSEPH ATKIN AND
STEPHEN TAROANIARA IN VENGEANCE FOR
WRONGS SUFFERED AT THE HANDS OF
EUROPEANS
BY SAVAGE MEN WHOM HE LOVED AND FOR
WHOSE SAKE HE GAVE UP HOME AND
COUNTRY
AND FRIENDS DEARER THAN HIS LIFE
LORD
JESUS
GRANT THAT WE MAY LIVE TO THEE
LIKE HIM AND STAND IN OUR LOT
WITH HIM BEFORE THY THRONE
AT THE END OF DAYS AMEN

This is the text on a memorial at Patteson cross on the A30 main road at Ottery St. Mary near Exeter in Devon.

Christian missionaries have received much criticism during the last half of the twentieth century, being accused of spiritual and cultural imperialism, ethnocide and other fallacious crimes. The truth is different. The critics often suffer from a subtle form of racism assuming native peoples to be ignorant, easily led, simpletons lacking intelligence, judgement, subtlety and discernment, who have been deceived by manipulative Missionaries. It is implied that if only the natives had the wisdom of the superior intellect of the European secularist to guide them they would not be taken in. Christian missionaries regarding all humanity as created in the image of God and that no one was excluded from the gospel of God's redemptive love, thought differently, treated them differently and managed to avoid the worst forms of scientific racism that emerged from the middle of the nineteenth century.

Also the critics of missionaries are often lost in romantic sentimentality regarding native cultures. The noble savage corrupted by the missionary is a myth. It is true that the missionaries regarded some aspects of native culture with horror and sought to bring changes – changes brought about by persuasion, preaching and the influence of the Christian God. Missionaries had no guns, no police and often the civil power (if there was one) was unsympathetic to the missionary and unsupportive.

Less than 200 years ago cannibalism was common in much of the under developed world and practiced widely in the

South Pacific. No more so than in New Zealand. In the late 1700s stories of ship's crews being massacred and eaten by the native Maoris horrified the northern hemisphere making New Zealand feared and avoided. The account of Samuel Marsden who arrived in New Zealand in 1814 as a missionary to the northern tribes is a remarkable story of selflessness, courage and love for the Maoris. He together with other dedicated Christians within 20 years planted mission stations all over both islands, often in the teeth of hostility. It took something like fifty years, which included two major wars between the settlers and the natives, for the civilising efforts of Christian teaching to persuade the Maoris that cannibalism was wrong and for them to embrace the gospel of forgiveness instead of their custom of 'tapu' where a wrong was unpardonable and must be revenged by death.

BISHOP PATTESON

A vivid and clear example of the positive impact of the Christian missionary is the story of Bishop Patteson. For years in the fairly lawless South Pacific white men, known as 'Blackbirders', had preyed on the natives of the islands either by deceit or kidnapping and had taken young men to the sugar plantations of Queensland and Fiji. In the 1870s it was such a serious problem that the islanders considered any European vessel to be a 'Blackbirder'. One of these notorious vessels disguised to look like Patteson's benign mission schooner 'Southern Cross', had been spreading havoc, kidnapping and murdering, in the New Hebrides islands in early September 1871. So when the Bishop actually turned up a few days after the 'Blackbirder' had left and went ashore on the island of Nukapu the natives enraged and eager for revenge brutally murdered him and two colleagues. Patteson's murder shocked the authorities in Australia and Britain into action and the *Pacific Islanders Protection Act of 1872* quickly passed through Parliament. This Act empowered the Royal Navy to hunt down and suppress 'Blackbirding'. The result was that local warfare and cannibalism was eradicated and a peaceful South Pacific emerged, such that, for example, the Gilbert Islands (now Kiribati) were governed for over fifty years by only about a dozen officials.

In the twenty first century missionaries are as active as ever going out into all the world, but it is an activity which causes much embarrassment to the secular atheistic community who cannot explain how ordinary people will devote their time, money, energy and their lives to the Christian gospel.

The missionary movement in its modern form operating over the last two hundred years, has revealed itself as a priceless gift to the whole world including the Americas, the Pacific, Africa and the East as well as Britain. Here are some more examples from Victorian times up to date.

JAMES CHALMERS

James Chalmers died a martyr's death in 1901 at the hands of pagan natives of Papua New Guinea whose cannibalistic rituals demanded human sacrifice. He was clubbed to death and eaten. He had worked for twenty five years bringing the Christian Gospel to the benighted man eating people of this unexplored remote island. A man of great courage, Chalmers lack of fear must have been a great factor of success in his hazardous work. He disarmed men by boldly going amongst them unarmed.

Papua New Guinea, one of the largest islands in the world, was in the 1870s largely unexplored and fearsomely uninviting. It was populated by countless mutually hostile tribes whose aggression climaxed in cannibalism. James and Jane Chalmers together with native missionaries from Rarotonga and their wives made their first home in Suau (or Stacey Island), where they found themselves surrounded by swarms of cannibals wearing human bones for ornaments. Chambers made it clear that he came among them in peace pointing out that they came with no weapons. In the spring of 1878 Chalmers, known as Tamate to the natives, sailed along the coast from east to west, visiting one hundred and five villages, of which ninety had never before seen a white man. He made extended journeys inland, always unarmed, either on foot or by canoe following the course of winding streams. He eventually planted a chain of mission stations, manned by Polynesian teacher-evangelists, along the south coast of Papua New guinea. In each place he made the first dangerous contact and stayed until the Papuans were reasonably friendly.

Chalmers was a man overwhelmed with conviction of God's love for humanity. He knew it for himself and expended his life telling the most depraved and benighted people of God's invitation, "Come to me". He constantly used the biblical text from Revelation 22 verse 17.

The Spirit and the Bride say, Come.
And let him that heareth say, Come.

And let him that is athirst come.
And whosoever will, let him take the water of life freely.

The author Robert Louis Stevenson, who met Chalmers in Polynesia described him as, "a man nobody can see and not love. A big stout wildish looking man, iron grey, with big bold eyes and a deep furrow down each cheek, with no humbug, plenty of courage and a love of adventure. He has plenty of faults like the rest of us but he is as big as a church".

HUDSON TAYLOR

"China is not to be won for Christ by quiet, ease-loving men and women … The stamp of men and women we need is such as will put Jesus, China, and souls first and foremost in everything and at every time—even life itself must be secondary."

James Hudson Taylor was a missionary to China. He founded the China Inland Mission which at his death in 1905 included 205 mission stations with over 800 missionaries, and 125,000 Chinese Christians.

Hudson Taylor arrived at Shanghai a fervent 21 year old impatient to proclaim the Christian gospel. So eager was he that in order to be better accepted he adopted Chinese clothes and even the pigtail. This passionate young man was not happy with most missionaries he worked with; he believed they were "worldly" and spent too much time with English businessmen and diplomats. So within months of arriving, and the native language still a challenge, Taylor, set off for the interior. He established a church in Ningpo which in four years had 21 members.

Hudson Taylor became convinced that a special organization was needed to evangelize the interior of China so he planned to recruit 24 missionaries: two for each of the 11 unreached inland provinces and two for Mongolia. It would increase the number of China missionaries by 25 percent. He established a new mission, which he called the China Inland Mission (CIM) and it had a number of distinctive features; its missionaries would have no guaranteed salaries nor could they appeal for funds; they would simply trust God to supply their needs; furthermore, its missionaries would adopt Chinese dress and then press the gospel into the China interior. Between his work ethic and his absolute trust in God (despite never soliciting funds, the CIM grew and prospered), he inspired thousands to forsake the comforts of the West to bring the glorious gospel to the vast and unknown interior of China.[42]

Hudson Taylor wrote, "At home you can never know what it is to be alone – absolutely alone, amidst thousands, without one friend, one companion, everyone looking on you with curiosity, with contempt, with suspicion or with dislike. Thus to learn what it is to be despised and rejected of man – of those you wish to benefit, your motives not understood but suspected – thus to learn what it is to have nowhere to lay your head; and then to have the love of Jesus applied to your heart by the Holy Spirit – His holy, self-denying love, which led Him to suffer this and more than this – for me this is precious, this is worth coming for."

---

[42] Most of this is from Christianhistory.net**h**

MARY SLESSOR

Mary Kingsley, the globe trotting niece of the author Charles Kingsley, arrived in Okoyong in what today is Southern Nigeria. She came by canoe and along remote jungle tracks to meet Ma Akambo. Mary a confirmed agnostic, like her father, and an avid believer in Darwin, had braved the dangerous rivers, swamps and jungles of tropical Africa to meet the renowned missionary Mary Slessor known to the native peoples as Ma Akambo. Mary Kingsley was concerned that missionaries were guilty of erasing native customs and culture. But native customs and superstition brought savage brutality to too many of the tribal people.

Mary Slessor in love with her devoted and faithful saviour fell in love with the people of the Calabar coast. It was here that much of the earlier slave trade had flourished. Witchcraft dominated the land and superstition was rife. When a chief died many people were murdered and his wives were strangled. Blood sacrifices were offered to the Juju spirits. Guilt was determined by poison being administered; if the accused lived he was innocent, if he died guilt was assumed. When twins were born they were always killed and the mother was banished to the bush to usually die, as it was believed that the devil had conceived one and as it was not possible to know which one both must die. Mary Slessor is purported to have said, "Oh, Mary Kingsley! How is it possible for you, a woman of intelligence, to suggest that it were better if this demon worship were preserved, and the natives left in what you call their innocence. The lovely customs that you so much admire are an unending horror."

Mary Slessor's passion was to introduce benighted people to their creator and redeemer who could rescue them from this darkness. Jesus Christ was all to her and his promise of his power and constant presence enabled her to confront these powers of evil in an extraordinary way. Whenever, she heard of the birth of twins she got hold of them as quickly as possible and her house was a sanctuary for those she rescued and many grew up to be a blessing to her and evidence to the superstitious natives that twins were a blessing from God. Up to 1890 she had saved over 50 twins.

Mary Slessor's activities, her preaching, her healing work, her influence on many local rulers who were often violently hostile towards each other was instrumental in bringing peace, prosperity and the release from fear to an extensive area of West Africa. And after 39 years in Africa she died at Calabar in 1915.

PETER and LINDA DAVEY

Catherine is an attractive and confident young woman of nineteen who comes from the town of Nakuru in Northern Kenya. Here is her story in Linda Davey's own words, "We expect Catherine to go on and make the most of her skills and abilities. Things were not always so rosy for her. We first met Catherine when she was about eleven, playing and wandering around the Nakuru rubbish dump. At that time she was living at home with her Mum and the rest of the children. She had an older sister who was sick with aids, we began to visit the home and assisted them. Unfortunately the sister died soon after.

Catherine and her younger sister Julia joined our programme and began to go to school and receive one square meal a day. However it wasn't long after that her mother also fell ill and soon afterwards she died. At this point the grandmother, Esther, took over the care of the children. She had no husband and depended on scavenging from the dump for her daily bread. Nevertheless she took the children in and did her best.

Catherine's mother's final request to us had been that we might look after her girls when she was gone. Getting Catherine through school became a priority for us.

She is a bright girl and despite missing some years of primary education she caught up with her classmates and after obtaining good marks in her primary examinations she was judged to be eligible for secondary school. It must be said that she grabbed the opportunity with both hands and has never looked back. She loved going to boarding school, as you can imagine living with more privileged pupils was a real eye opener, after a life spent in squalor. She is always near the top of her class and conducts herself well. It is always strange to see this smart, clean, well fed young woman when she is on her way back home in the holidays, trudging up the hill to her Grandmother's house in scruffy old Hilton.

After five years in boarding schools in Nairobi and Nakuru district she is now ready to take her final exams. She would love to have the chance to go on to university, but it is more likely that she will now seek employment or training. Whatever is decided over the coming months one thing is certain, this young woman is in a privileged position when it comes to taking her place in the world.

Grandma Esther by the way is now a stalwart of our grannies group and amongst other things shares in the benefits of the knitting group and the pig rearing programs. Julia meanwhile remains in the programme and is coming towards the end of her eight years of primary school."

Peter Davey worked for many years as a minister of a church in a small English town and simultaneously spent part of his time training Christian pastors in Kenya. Eventually in the mid 1990s his commitment in Africa grew to such an extent that he and Linda moved their home to Nakuru. While Peter's training work took him all over Kenya Linda used her nursing skills to bring God's love, care and healing to the poorest people who were only able to survive by scavenging on the town rubbish dump. Her 'Rags to riches' program was a godsend where at any one time they might support up to 15 children in primary school to provide uniforms, shoes, books and a daily lunchtime meal; four in secondary boarding school; one in a Special School and one in secondary day school. The program also supports grannies who meet on Fridays, knitting away and rearing their latest litter of piglets. Saturday mornings are busy with 150 or so youngsters from all over the slum area turning up for games, songs and a bite to eat.

The African climate coupled with the disease risk associated with working on a rubbish dump has taken its toll on their health. Peter and Linda have now retired, but maintain close contacts with all the programs they have worked with in Kenya. The work continues and is run more and more by local people.

* * *

People seem to have a built-in hunger for the divine and eagerly respond to the Christian message of rescue from spiritual darkness through repentance and God's love and mercy. This is universal and wherever the Gospel is preached people always respond. Even where tyranny suppresses the message people respond. The most spiritually desolate places are cultures like that prevailing in Britain in the early twenty first century where intellectual idolatry and self worship on the part of those dominating society infiltrate all aspects of national life, excluding through ridicule and direct opposition any ideas which do not meet their secular agenda. This is totalitarianism in a dangerous form whose harvest is desolation and misery on a grand scale.

However, if the Christian Good News is true, then God inspired men and women will express the message of reconciliation between man and God in ways which address the needs and aspirations of the age. After all the sneers, disdain, ridicule and threats directed at Christians are nothing new[43] and pale into insignificance compared with what was endured by James Chalmers, Bishop Patteson and many others.

---

[43] The Bible - John chapter 15 verse 20; Matthew chapter 5 verse 11

Last Chapter

HOW DID WE GET HERE?

What more oft, in nations grown corrupt and by their vices brought to servitude, than to love bondage more than liberty, bondage with ease than strenuous liberty.[44]

How is that Britain, the most successful nation in the history of the world, has come to the state where we get our culture from the USA, get our politics from Brussels and are getting to the stage where our religion comes from Arabia?

At the end of the Second World War three factors coincided which have had an impact on Britain with which the country is still grappling. Firstly the war required that the state controlled most material aspects of life in order that all resources were focused on defeating our enemies. Secondly, in 1945 the Labour party was elected to power and thirdly the granting of independence to India quickly

---

[44] Samson Agonistes – John Milton

followed by most other colonies saw many able and gifted colonial administrators return to Britain.

For the duration of the war the nation was willing to delegate immense powers to the government and a virtual dictatorship was accepted as a price worth paying to ensure victory; a victory which would allow British freedoms to be secured and restored. The nation which fought with a united purpose for 6 years grew used to receiving and obeying commands and directives from the government; a government which was on the side of the people.

The election of 1945 brought to power a socialist government which was ideologically committed to extending state control of the nation, nationalising much of industry and the health service, introducing the welfare state, and promising to abolish poverty.

In 1947 India became independent and many gifted administrators returned to Britain. Hundreds more returned from many other colonies all over the world over the next few years and most took up positions in the rapidly expanding government service, both local and national. They brought with them the paternalistic governing culture which had served them reasonably well overseas, but had become outdated. These outdated ideas, which would no longer be accepted by the ex colonies, fitted perfectly the philosophy the new Labour government imposed on an exhausted, regimented and bankrupt Britain.

In parallel with the expansion of government was the growth of atheistic secular humanism and this growth mirrored the accelerating decline of formal religion. This rapid decline can be illustrated by a remark attributed to Harold Macmillan when Prime Minister in the early 1960s when asked to comment on a moral question he replied, "I leave that to the Bishops…"[45] This is not an answer any politician would dream of giving forty years later. Almost weekly a crime, often sexual, is committed and a politician promises, "lessons will be learnt….., an independent enquiry will be setup….., new legislation will be brought in….." Much sound and fury together with socially restrictive legislation and then we wait for the next incident. Impotence dominates; masked by fervent, expensive and often useless activity.

Coupled with the growth in secularism and the decline in traditional religion and morality is the retreat from truth into a bastion of pride and self delusion. This has led to Britain losing her way; from being the paramount world power to insignificant province of Europe.

What is the reason for this?

Is there a reason or is this just the inevitable decline which all ancient and worn out nations must endure? As with individuals so with nations, with old age comes death? Inevitability which is closely related to fatalism has never been an English or Christian characteristic so the reason for national decline is worth exploring and facing.

Chapter 4 opened with the quote from Piers Brendon where he wrote, "The empire made Britain great. Without

---

[45]   Also attributed to Macmillan – "If people want a sense of purpose they should get it from their archbishop. They should certainly not get it from their politicians".

it, as its statesmen and service chiefs privately reiterated, the mother country would be an insignificant island anchored forlornly off the coast of Europe." Of course, it would be more accurate to say that Great Britain made the empire! Confidence, freedom of movement, inventiveness and growing wealth brought the empire about almost by accident. It was not a planned enterprise.[46] But in the middle of the nineteenth century again three factors coincided.

By the mid 1800s Britain was at the peak of her industrial strength. She was the workshop of the world, her inventors were breaking new ground, her scientists and engineers were overcoming every obstacle, her navy sailed wherever it wished on the globe and confidence was boiling over into pride. Then in 1857 came the Indian mutiny which gave this confidence a massive blow. It was suppressed most viciously and a sad gulf grew between the British governing race and the native Indians which engendered suspicion and mistrust. And thirdly, in 1859 Darwin published his "Origin of Species".

This cataclysmic book promoted the idea of evolution, natural selection and the survival of the fittest. The fittest of course meant the European powers with Britain in the fore. Darwin and his teaching struck a blow at the root of the Christian culture of Britain. The Bible opens with the words, "*In the beginning God created the heavens and earth*", but Darwinism said, "No he didn't! It all happened through random molecular changes over

---

[46]   In 1862 the Colonial Office employed 48 staff, who only worked in the afternoons! – Piers Brendon The Decline and Fall of the British Empire p 73.

countless millions of years." Ritualistic religion had a diminishing appeal to thinking people and as a twentieth century writer has said, "Darwin made it possible to be an intellectually fulfilled atheist"[47]. Atheistic Secular Humanism (ASH) has made immense inroads since this time and this belief system now dominates the intellectual landscape in Britain. It is a world view which is spiritually sterile and has led to destructive ideologies which have brought immense suffering to humanity. It is also responsible for the perverted moral theory of eugenics. It was this institutionalised and intellectually justified sense of superiority which began to pervade the western world including Britain. It also had a corrosive effect on the British empire where it became intellectually respectable to despise less fortunate races just when the curse of slavery was being consigned to history. The decline of Britain can be measured from this time.

This mixture of pride and fear coupled with a self centric philosophical world view took the zest out of the nation. The 'God is dead' doctrine which flowed from Darwinism struck thinking Christians of every denomination a stunning blow. Since this time they have been on the back foot, avoiding taking the Bible seriously, taking an apologetic tone whenever their beliefs are challenged, leaving the moral and ethical territory to the impotent, incompetent and intolerant alternative world view and sometimes retreating into ritualistic obscurantism. This sad state of Christian leadership has been the norm for so long that clergymen are caricatured as feebleminded, shallow, do-gooders and has suppressed and depressed

---

[47] Richard Dawkins from his book *The Blind Watchmaker*

good committed passionate men and women and prevented them from boldly presenting their beliefs in the intellectual marketplace.

But it is atheistic secular humanism which is bankrupt. ASH is burnt out. It is useless because it has no spiritual dimension; it has no mechanism for addressing failures except to demand more and more state money; it is in intense denial about its own limitations; it assumes that impotent hand wringing and pompous empty words are a satisfactory response to any event outside its control; it has no moral base to measure right and wrong; it is a philosophy without hope.

An example of the bankruptcy of this world view is how Britain and other nations saturated by atheistic secular humanism responded to the various events which made national and world news during the last week of November 2008.

The Bombay terrorist attacks.

The Islamic terrorist attacks on several targets in Bombay are firstly a spiritual problem. The ASH two dimensional world view denying any spiritual facet to life, concentrating on materialism and the survival of the fittest leaves minority groups and the poor feeling rejected which fuels a growing sense of grievance. There is a desert-like spiritual vacuum which is being filled by extremists, some of whom are eager to carry out terrorist attacks on the 'fittest' pouring out their rage using unreasonable violence. ASH cannot communicate with these people.

Zimbabwe Cholera outbreak.

This disease is fairly easy to control using standard techniques and in the modern world with normal hygienic procedures it need never breakout. However, in Zimbabwe more than 500 hundred people have died from cholera in three months and many more a likely to die because of government breakdown. An incompetent government based on Marxism has not received the contempt it deserves because the secular states, not only Britain, Europe and the USA, but also almost all those in southern Africa, share the same world view as the Mugabe regime and do not have the moral weight to demand improvements. This moral degeneration is illustrated by the attitude of the ASH nations to the Congo, Sudan, Rwanda, North Korea and other failed states.

Sheffield man jailed for fathering nine children by his daughters.

Much moral indignation came from people in high places regarding this abuse. The Prime Minister was 'outraged' by this 'unspeakable' abuse perpetrated against the women and said, "If the system has failed, we will change the system". An 'independent review' is investigating the health professionals, police and social services. There being no absolute right or wrong, then any desire anyone has, however perverted, is legitimate until it goes beyond a certain ill defined line and then the humbug machine is switched on. This politically correct line is a moving line descending all the time towards depravity. 18 month old Baby P was murdered by his mother and current 'boy friend'. The inquiry has been ordered and the social services are in the firing line. Good, committed and able professional men and woman are being expected to deliver the impossible by a society corrupted by ASH. The state's response is to introduce the "Contact" data base holding records of all children in England and will cost countless millions. So to avoid another high profile child abuse case coming to light officials can be disciplined for not keeping correct records or the parents jailed for not permitting the data to be collected. This is where moral relativism takes us.

Sexually harassed female soldier gets record damages.

This is another example of moral relativism. A wounded soldier who lost two limbs while on active service received £140,000 in compensation. The sexually harassed female soldier received £180,000; a considerable portion for hurt feelings. This is also moral manipulation whereby a social movement with a sense of victimhood demands that society generally compensates for a perceived offence. ASH, lacking all sense of proportion is in thrall to extreme and strident forces.

Police raid on MP's office and home.

And so it goes on......

The Christian community has become so demoralized since the mid 1800s that the demoralized state has become the normal state. Christians don't venture into the intellectual marketplace as believing Christians and when they infrequently do, it is as secularists on ASH's terms.

They take an apologetic stance and fit into the mould determined for them by the secular world view. This mould is so constraining for a believing Christian that is like keeping an eagle in a canary cage. And the result is depression and burnout for so many of their leaders. Growing out from what is essentially an abdication by Christians is the decline of public and private virtue and its resulting misery which is so prevalent in twenty first century Britain.

But times are changing. It is time for the British to open their eyes to look at their history and see how their country has blessed the whole world in countless ways over many centuries. It is time to face the fact that the secular experiment has not worked and accept reality and humbly move on.

It is not possible to make a silk purse out of a pigs ear.

Epilogue

WHERE DO WE GO FROM HERE?

See, darkness covers the earth and thick darkness is over the peoples,

But the LORD rises upon you and His glory appears over you.[48] ...

It is not possible to make a silk purse out of a pig's ear. It is not possible to create or preserve a culture or civilisation out of ASHes.

The Christian community is stirring. They are 'pushing the boundaries'[49]; not downwards towards ever more degrading levels of behaviour, but pushing upwards against lowering standards in so many walks of life. The thankless task of supporting the marginalized, disadvantaged, exploited people which requires love,

---

[48] The Bible - Isaiah Chapter 60 verse 2

[49] Early twenty first century has many similar buzz phrases, such as 'it must not be allowed to happen again' said almost daily by a government minister after a serious failure in a public service.

patience, self sacrifice and longsuffering is increasingly being undertaken by the church. This is a job the Salvation Army has always done and has become more vital with a growing number of needy people who figure little in the welfare state's world. The churches are also providing professional and secure rehabilitation for battered women who often need tender long term support to enable them to live fulfilled lives. There are many more examples..

The church was content to relinquish such functions to the state in 1945, but the 'brave new world' has not materialised as the state is a poor provider and cannot deliver.

The church preaching the Christian gospel is uniquely placed to offer love and kindness; qualities in short supply in the modern world.

Christians are rediscovering their obligation to care for those less fortunate, to obey their master and to realise that they cannot love and show compassion by proxy. It is hard work, uncomfortable and challenging to received wisdom, but we have a God who loves us, who is omnipotent and has said he will never leave us or forsake us; who is interested in every small detail of our lives. He is re-equipping his church.

Our confidence in our God is growing and one day perhaps will be sufficient to proclaim the greatest news the world has ever heard in the open unforgiving intellectual market place.

The word of the LORD is right and true;
He is faithful in all he does.
The LORD loves righteousness and justice;
the earth is full of His unfailing love.
By the word of the LORD were the heavens made,
their starry host by breath of his mouth.
He gathers the waters of the sea into jars;
He puts the deep into storehouses.
Let all the earth fear the LORD;
let all the people of the world revere him.
For he spoke, and it came to be;
He commanded and it stood firm.
The LORD foils the plans of the nations;
He thwarts the purposes of the peoples.
But the plans of the LORD stand firm forever,
the purpose of his heart through all generations.
Blessed is the nation whose God is the LORD.[50]

---

[50]   The Bible - Psalm 33 verse 4+

Bibliography - books

Paradise Lost by John Milton

Samson Agonistes by John Milton

The Dark Valley by Piers Brendon published by Random House London

The Decline and Fall of the British Empire by Piers Brendon published by Jonathan Cape London

Wealth and Poverty of Nations by David Landes published by W.W Norton and Co New York

The Government of the British Empire by E. Jenks published by John Murray London

The Men who ruled India by Philip Mason published by Rupa and Co New Delhi

Sir Bartle Frere and his Times by Rekha Ranade, published by Mittal Publications New Delhi

Confessions of a Thug by Philip Meadows Taylor published by Rupa and Co New Delhi

Mapping of an Empire by Matthew Edney published by University of Chicago Press

The White Nile by Alan Whitehead published by Hamish Hamilton London

Pattern of Island by Arthur Grimble published by John Murray London

The Story of Mankind by Hendrick Van Loon

Flushed with Pride by Wallace Reyburn published by Pavilion Books London

The Blind Watchmaker by Richard Dawkins

Giants of the Missionary Trail was originally published by Scripture Press, Book Division, [1954].

Fistful of heroes by John Pollock and published by Christian Focus Publications

African Missionary Heroes and Heroines by H.K.W. Kumm. New York: MacMillan Company, 1917.

The Bible

Bibliography – Internet references

www.as.ua.edu/ant/Faculty/murphy/436/pomo.htm

www.infoplease.com/ipa/A0107875.html

www.greatsite.com/timeline-english-bible-history/john-wycliffe.html

www.newadvent.org/cathen/13333b.htm

www.groups.dcs.st-and.ac.uk/~history/Biographies/Galileo.html

www.reformation.org/bart.html

www.british-civil-wars.co.uk/biog/waller.htm

www.fordham.edu/halsall/mod/1679habeascorp.html

www.bagchee.com/books.php?id=18324

www.archive.org/stream/generaljohnjacob00shanrich#page/n5/mode/2up

www.indianetzone.com/3/lord_john_lawrence.htm

www.sscnet.ucla.edu/southasia/History/British/jolly_good.html

www.victorianweb.org/history/frere.html

http://bvml.org/webmaster/sleeman.html

www.guyana.org/features/guyanastory/chapter46.html

www.bbc.co.uk/history/british/empire_seapower/antislavery_06.shtml

http://htc.churchinsight.com/Group/Group.aspx?id=31509

www.wluml.org/english/pubs/pdf/occpaper/OCP-07.pdf

www.alanwatson.org/somersets_case.pdf

www.bbc.co.uk/history/british/abolition/royal_navy_article_01.shtml

www.brycchancarey.com/abolition/clarkson.htm

www.bbc.co.uk/history/british/abolition/william_wilberforce_article_01.shtml

www.cottontimes.co.uk/hedley.htm

www.derbyshireuk.net/whitworth.html

www.spartacus.schoolnet.co.uk/RApease.html

http://www-groups.dcs.st-and.ac.uk/~history/Biographies/Faraday.html

www.mlahanas.de/Greeks/HeroAndLoon.htm

http://people.bath.ac.uk/hssdcg/Michael_Faraday.html

www.uh.edu/engines/epi157.htm

www.devonperspectives.co.uk/babbage.html

www.technology.niagarac.on.ca/people/mcsele/newcomen.htm

www.swopnet.com/engr/londonsewers/londontext1.html

www.pittdixon.go-plus.net/whitworth/whitworth.htm

www.spartacus.schoolnet.co.uk/RAstockton.htm

www.crossness.org.uk/sites/20020715PJK/problems.htm

www.rigb.org/contentControl?pg=4&filter=pd&action=detail&section=1391

http://jmm.aaa.net.au/articles/14542.htm

www.railcentre.co.uk/stockton/stocktonmenu.htm

www.authorama.com/story-of-mankind-25.html

http://inventors.about.com/od/nstartinventors/a/Newcomen_2.htm

www.locos-in-profile.co.uk/Articles/Early_Locos/early3.html

www.englishlanguageguide.com/english/facts/history/

www.talkfootball.co.uk/guides/history_of_football.html

www.britainexpress.com/History/pastimes/cricket.htm

www.visitbritain.ca/campaigns/premier-league/football-in-britain/the-home-of-football.aspx

www.rugbyfootballhistory.com/originsofrugby.htm

http://justus.anglican.org/resources/bio/73.html

www.wholesomewords.org/biography

www.christianitytoday.com/ch/131christians/
missionaries/htaylor.html?start=1

www.wholesomewords.org/missions/giants/biochalmers.
html

www.teara.govt.nz/en/1966/marsden-samuel/1

www.wholesomewords.org/biography/biorpslessor.html

www.1914-1918.net/faq.htm

www.theage.com.au/world/hundreds-die-in-zimbabwe-
cholera-outbreak-20081129-6new.html